◆ <u>Smart Relationships</u> ◆

Joan M. Chamberlain, MS, CPC
joanevrard@gmail.com

Smart
Relationships

Probe Your Deeper Self,
Create a Loving
Relationship

Joan M. Chamberlain, M.S.

Evelany Publishing
St. Louis

Published by Evelany Publishing

III

Library of Congress Control Number: 2003114994

For information, address:

Evelany Publishing
P. O. Box 485
Ballwin, MO 63022

Cover design by Ed Berns
Interior design by Donna Baden Reeves

ISBN 0-9674923-0-0
Printed in the United States

ACKNOWLEDGMENTS

To my clients: I'm indebted to each of you because you've trusted me with your deepest personal challenges. Thanks for asking the questions over the years that this book is meant to answer. I am grateful to have known every one of you.

Thanks to my friends, who graciously read parts of the manuscript along the way. They gave me solid suggestions for improvement, and were always, always encouraging and enthusiastic.

Two professional writers were especially important for me in my early writing. Hal Zina Bennett, who is a published author of many books, as well as an editor, and writing consultant. He helped me with the original outline and gave structure to my scattered notes. He provided direction that encouraged me, especially initially, as I tried to find my way. Jan Gilmore, 5th Brick Productions, helped edit as I developed the manuscript. Thanks to them both. Their knowledge was invaluable.

Thanks to my family: son, David, daughter-in-law Michelle, and grandsons, Andrew and Anthony, who for years have put up with references to "the book" without any tangible evidence that it actually existed.

Lastly, thanks to my daughter, Leah, and my granddaughter, Tiffany, for their ceaseless patience, enthusiasm and help, as they lived with me while I struggled to "get my words right."

ॐॐॐ

Miscellaneous

♦♦♦ In trying to make this book clear and easy to read, I've used the term "he" generically when referring to both women and men. I wanted to use a more neutral pronoun but in trying others, I found they made the writing awkward and unclear. The copy is not intended to be sexist. ◆◆◆

◆◆◆ The stories and examples in this book are based on the experiences of real people. However, all names and identifying facts have been changed. In all cases, the author has used composite examples to protect the privacy of individuals. ◆◆◆

ॐॐॐ

To Jeannie Moskoff: A special salute to a special person.
Jeannie, thank you very much.

Contents

PREFACE

This book has been in the making for some years. It actually came about because I had nothing in written form to hand my clients when they wanted to know more about the personality concept that was so helpful to them in our sessions together.

The book started as a group of handouts and charts, that I developed to give my clients some quick data about communication and defenses. I thought they would make a decent-sized booklet. But, the information seemed to grow and take on a life of its own.

Finally, about five years ago I decided to pull all of my material together as a book. My husband's death and other family responsibilities stretched out my final writing time. But, it's finished now, and I hope that it will be helpful to you.

ॐॐॐ

My love affair with the Adlerian model of therapy started 25 years ago in my first year as a graduate counseling student at Butler University in Indianapolis. There's a course early in the program that introduces the student to different counseling "models." These models present different theories of how personality develops. The would-be therapist picks one that he feels he can use to best serve his client.

When I started graduate school, I was in my middle thirty's. I had already had a career in the corporate world and I had taught high school for eight years. I had been married for 12 years and had a son. My value system and my philosophy of life, including relationship with others, were already well established. When I read the Adlerian concepts, I knew I was "home." The whole approach felt right for me. It has faith in the individual person. It promotes respectful equality among all. It's optimistic and encouraging.

I love this model because it promotes both studying ourselves and relating to others with an attitude of respect, openness, and hope. The Adlerian goal is always to nudge the client toward more understanding and acceptance of self. This model teaches that when a person decides to alter unhealthy ideas and behaviors, he can do it. Eventually, through understanding and change, he can build a healthy inner power center. With it, he establishes healthy relationships and guides himself through life.

Also, I very much liked the description of the Adlerian therapist. He becomes a helping friend to the client by genuinely feeling and showing warmth and interest in him. The therapist is an equal fellow human being, not one who is superior. He shows the courage to "take on" life without fear that he will make mistakes. He is one who tries and tries again in life, always working towards improvement, not deluding himself that he should achieve perfection. He's active in expressing feelings and opinions. He encourages others to develop "social interest," that is, sharing themselves with others.

During his years as a doctor, the psychiatrist, Dr. Alfred Adler, founded the widely accepted school of Individual Psychology in the late 1890's. The main principles of the philosophy are: (1) Each person wants to "belong," to carve out a positive space in his original family, and then, gradually, in the adult world. Our personal roadblocks are social problems, that is, those of fitting in with other people. In other words, the difficulties we have are those of social interaction. (2) Each person is self-determining. We can decide what we will do; we are not victims. If we choose to change, we can. Even if we are powerless to change the situation we're in, we can still decide how we will react to it. (3) Our behavior has purpose, although we're not always aware of what it is. We are often led by our unconscious, much of which we do not know, since it is below the surface of our awareness. Only a part of our experiences are conscious. (4) We experience life subjectively. It is not what happens to us, but how we feel and think about it. (5) We are holistic. We are not parts to be understood or explained individually, but a whole person to be viewed as more than the sum of its parts. We can look for patterns in our actions and understand ourselves through them.

In studying people, one of Dr. Adler's conclusions was that people's behavior falls into one of four personality types:

Useful, Ruling, Avoiding and Getting. As he developed his concept and spoke about these types, he cautioned that they should never be used to label or judge people, but, instead, to understand and help.

In the early 1970's, Dr. Nira Kefir and then, Dr. Raymond Corsini, and Dr. William Pew, three Adlerian theorists, added to and expanded these personality types. They used the names Comfort, Pleasing, Control and Superiority. It is this model that I partially explain in this book.

Edith and Milton Dewey, Adlerian teachers, devised a personality chart using these types, and included it in a booklet called Basic Applications of Adlerian Psychology. This booklet was published by Don C. Dinkmeyer's company, CMTI Press, Coral Springs, Florida in 1978. I've expanded the original single chart, which contained all four types, into four individual ones. They're included in Chapter Three of this book. I've added the Core Belief sections as well as additional information in other sections of the chart.

Dr. Adler himself was a prime example of one who lived out his values of respecting, understanding, and helping others at every opportunity. His whole attitude in life and in teaching his Psychology was one that emphasized "social interest," a term he used to describe people sharing themselves with others and among all.

It is in the spirit of social interest that I offer this material. I've never seen anything to equal this Adlerian model of personality types for quickness and clarity. I hope it will help you, as it has helped my clients for the last twenty years, make more sense of your own self and enable you to cultivate loving relationships.

Ultimately, I believe we'll all create healthier and happier lives if we know that we can change our futures by changing our beliefs from the past. With one lifestyle change at a time, we can make ourselves, our families, and the world, a better place for all of us. I'm confident that if you try, you will succeed. Then, you'll have the power to fill your life and relationships with contentment and joy.

෩෩෩

Part One

About You

Courage isn't that we act because we feel no fear. Courage is facing fear and moving through it. Come on along.

ૐ   ૐ   ૐ

Chapter One

Come Along

*E*ach of us has an intense longing to connect with others, especially those we love. We want our relationships to be meaningful. We know that each of us has the ability to relate. Why is it then, that so many of us struggle with our relationships, especially our intimate ones? Why is it that we partners who love each other very, very much can't get along? A couple of reasons, I think. But, thankfully, these we can do something about.

First, we need to know ourselves. Because most of us are busy just coping with daily living, we react to life. We don't study it or ourselves in it. So, here we are trying to do life, without knowing where our actions come from, why we've chosen them, or what they symbolize.

On the other hand, when we decide to learn more, we move from a place of not knowing to understanding self. What's the payoff? As you watch yourself, you understand your behavior better. You aren't just reacting anymore; you know where your actions are coming from and why they're happening. Prior unknown pieces of you become apparent: your deepest core beliefs, the motives and behaviors your beliefs produce, and the clever ways you defend all of those. That's great, because to have a happy life and a loving relationship, you must know and accept yourself.

1

Here's another plus: whatever confusion or anxiety you've been feeling falls away. These recede into relief.

With this new self-awareness, you take the first step on an exciting journey with yourself: friendship. I invite you; come along.

৯৵৯৵৯৵

Earlier, I said that there are two things that prevent us from enjoying a good life. The first: we don't know who we are. The second: we don't know how to do intimate relationships.

Relationships are intricate, complex. We don't understand them: why they work, why they don't, when they don't, how to fix them. We don't know what will make our connections successful.

Yes, if you think about it, where can you learn to do smart, mutually rewarding relationships? These skills aren't taught anywhere. You might think that you learned them in your original home. But, if what you saw there wasn't healthy, you still may not be successful in your own adult partnerships.

Most partners I see are profoundly angry and feeling hopeless about each other. This is true, even though initially, they were deeply in love.

If you and your partner feel down and hopeless, I understand why. You're doing what you know how to do. You're doing what you believe is right. And yet, it isn't working. When you try to get through to your partner, you can't. He has long since tuned you out. And you, too, are closed. Except for the heavy, loaded silence or the awful screaming, your relationship has ceased. You fear that it will never be reclaimed, even though you still truly love each other.

So, what can you do to help your situation? You can get smart about how to do a strong, loving relationship. That means committing to: (1) learning how you came to be the person you are, getting to know yourself, (2) learning to be open and respectful with the one you love, and (3) learning how to

2

negotiate and compromise with each other. If you want to nourish your relationships, you need these skills.

Once you have awareness and knowledge, you can rebuild your relationship. As that rebuilding happens, you'll feel the love you initially felt for each other flow again. Just imagine how good it will be when you face your partner without anger. Trust can be rebuilt. True respect can grow, perhaps for the first time. Then, your love has a strong possibility for new depth. Your relationship may end up being better than ever.

You see, once you commit to understand and respect yourself, then you can commit to understand and respect those you choose to have in your life. If your partner chooses this also, together you can create a loving bond, the intimate, smart relationship that you each long for.

I invite you to come along and give yourself this gift of inner growth. Through it, be patient. Do not judge yourself. Understand that raising your awareness takes time.

Encourage yourself. You'll experience large payoffs: losing your anxiety and, eventually, enjoying a solid core of peace. The added reward: a healthy relationship appears because you finally "get it." Then, CELEBRATE your success.

ॐ   ॐ   ॐ

Big Ideas From Chapter One.

1.   *Encourage yourself on your journey to
knowing who you are.*

2.   *Acquire the skills you need to have a Smart
Relationship.*

Start growing today.

Our lives make deep sense only when we
open both our minds and our hearts.

   ❧   ❧   ❧

Chapter Two

Your Personality Types

How You Came To Be Who You Are.

*I*magine yourself when you were an infant, new on this earth. You were helpless. You couldn't take care of yourself. Your mother and father and perhaps, older siblings, helped you as you began your life's journey. They took care of you.

At about two or three months of age, after you settled on your sleeping and eating schedule, you began to study your new home and the people in it. You needed to figure out how to "fit in," how to "belong" in your family. Later, you would decide how to fit in with the world outside your home. You were on your way, learning to do life.

As you grew from infancy through toddlerhood and into preschool and kindergarten age, you unconsciously developed behaviors that made sense to you, given the activity you saw in your new home. You decided on how to fit in and belong by mixing the (1) messages you received from those around you with (2) other messages you got when <u>you</u> acted to satisfy your physical and emotional needs.

In other words, from birth until you were four or five, you watched your family members and interacted with them. From those moments, you unconsciously developed ideas about yourself, about others, and about the world. All together these ideas became your belief system. Since early childhood these beliefs have directed your behavior in a certain way.

We can make a couple of observations about your belief system. First you, like most children, were probably good at observing. From what you saw, you drew many right conclusions about how to be, how to belong in your family. So, many of your conscious and unconscious beliefs are healthy; they help you live a productive life.

But, because you were very young with no experience, you formed some wrong conclusions. So, some of the beliefs you own now about how you should "be" in life direct unhealthy behavior. These beliefs set you up for pain and failure.

Secondly, your conclusions came directly out of your family setting. If your family system operated in healthy ways, your collection of beliefs should be mostly healthy. But, if your family system functioned in unhealthy ways, some of your beliefs lead you astray. Right away, you can see that if you want to know yourself better, looking back objectively at your original family will help you. And, as a bonus, this can be really interesting.

Yes, it is amazing but true that you, like all of us, finished building most of your belief system by age five. It's true that this collection of ideas has directed your behavior from then until now. Further, this mostly unconscious belief system will guide you for the rest of your adult life unless you recognize it, acknowledge your healthy beliefs, and then modify or discard the unhealthy ones.

Is the idea of a belief system a discovery for you? It was for me. I often wondered why people behaved as they did. And I was curious about the differences between people, even as a child. I always respected the variations, but I didn't know why they were there.

We are each different because every one of us draws our own silent, individual conclusions about life and how to be in

6

it. Then, we act them out. My core beliefs and yours may be similar, but my emphasis on one or another belief may be different from yours. So, my behavior will take a little different direction. Or, you will own beliefs that I don't. Where you have specific beliefs, I have an empty hole. So, your whole direction will be different. And, if the opposite is true, so will my actions go another way. And so on. You see, our behavior isn't simply random. Behavior results from motive. Motive results from beliefs. It all starts with what you, the little person, decide.

Whatever your belief system, you're an intriguing package. And, truly unique.

There's more. You developed beliefs that manage your behavior in three distinct spaces in your life. These are: (1) how you should behave, (2) how you expect others to treat you and each other, and (3) how you expect the world to be.

Following this idea, as a little person you could have developed a positive, healthy group of beliefs like: (1) I will be active, not one who waits, (2) I expect others to treat me and each other respectfully, (3) the world is an interesting place. If you have these beliefs, your behavior is strong and healthy. You have few defenses.

On the other hand, you could have developed a darker, unhealthy group of beliefs, such as: (1) I'll wait and not initiate in life, (2) Others can't be trusted; I'm suspicious of them, (3) Life is uncertain, maybe even dangerous. If you have these beliefs, you hesitate before acting, or you don't act at all. You treat others and life cautiously. You have many defenses because you are afraid.

If you learn to observe behavior carefully, you can often tell what others believe. (Remember; actions come from beliefs.) And, if you use your own feelings as antennae, you can feel different emotions in the air. In other words, you can often see and feel the difference that comes from different belief collections. Why is awareness about these differences so important? If you want health for yourself, you must be able to recognize it.

Personality Types.

Over a hundred years ago Alfred Adler, the great psychiatrist and originator of the Individual Psychology theory, suggested that if we look closely at our own and other's behavior, we see four distinct personality types. Just generally these types are really interesting. But, when you use them to learn who you are, they can be downright fascinating. You can see where your behavior comes from. Then, you can use them to predict behavior: yours and other's.

Of course, none of us can be described exactly. We are each too complex for that. But, my clients have great success in using these types as guides. You can give yourself the same gift by using them to learn about you.

So, what are the personality types that will help you know yourself better? There are four: (1) Comfort, (2) Pleasing, (3) Control, and (4) Superiority. You, like most of us, use all four of these types of behavior in your daily life. Thus, you use some Comfort, some Pleasing, some Control, and some Superiority in your actions every day.

But you, like most people, probably have two "favorite" types. Most of your behavior comes from two deep pools of beliefs. Certainly, you own beliefs from the other two types, but you probably don't act them out as frequently. If you observe yourself closely, you'll see that you're using your top two style choices consistently every day in everything you do, including your interactions with others.

Identifying your two stronger and two weaker personality types provides a quick understanding of yourself. If you can nail down your strongest styles, you're definitely ahead in your goal to know yourself. You can use your new awareness NOW to make your life what you want it to be.

彦彦彦

Remember, the two types you use the most answer your long ago unconscious question: How can I best "fit in" and "belong" in my family? So, your current behaviors tell how you see yourself "fitting in" and "belonging" now in your adult world.

ॐॐॐ

More Depth.

Let me tell you a little about each type. By looking at these short descriptions, you can get a feel for which styles are your strongest. Much more detail comes in the next two chapters.

The Comfort Type.

You're a Comfort person if staying comfortable in every way: physically, emotionally, intellectually, and socially, is your top priority. So, you do what keeps you comfortable. You sleep, watch TV, go to the movies, shop, eat, sit in the hot tub, drink, and so on. You want that feel-good feeling right now, as instantly and as consistently, all-the-time as you can get it.

You're charming and appealing and usually easy-going. You may have a bubbly personality (that's your active charm) or you may be laid-back (the old-shoe, passive kind of charm). You're spontaneous and fun-loving. You're friendly and predictable. You mind your own business and don't make demands on others, especially if you're passive. You're probably diplomatic. These qualities are some of your positives.

Here are some of your negatives. You avoid expectations. They create stress and pressure, which interfere with your comfort. You don't take on responsibility; you've spent your energy on comfort. You're usually bored or impatient with anything that doesn't directly concern you. You may not be reliable with time or money. You probably don't set goals. Why not? You perceive goals as work and work is uncomfortable.

A few of your core beliefs are:

1. I don't deal with reality or responsibility when it's unpleasant.

2. Others will do it, whatever it is.
3. Life must be comfortable; it must feel good.

The unconscious goal of this style is to remain comfortable, no matter what.

The Pleasing Type.

You are a Pleasing person if you are happiest when you're making others happy. That's your top priority. You do so mainly by taking care of them. Because connection is so important to you, you behave as others expect you to. You are likely to volunteer because you are extra-responsible about doing what others want. You're very busy.

You are friendly and considerate. You're respectful of others. You're sympathetic and empathic with them. You take care of other's physical, emotional, intellectual, social and sometimes, financial needs, too. You do this because you want those you love to be happy. To this end, you're also flexible and cooperative. You're probably talented too, because you'll learn anything you need to, to give people what they want. These qualities are some of your positives.

Here are some of your negatives. Talented or not, your versatility isn't benefiting you. You're too busy focusing on others. You may not even know what you need or want, because you don't have time to think about it. And if, by chance, you have figured out what you want, you feel guilty and selfish for thinking about it. You don't develop your independence because you don't have time; you're too busy serving. You can't conceive of not being attached through giving and service to the one you love.

A few of your core beliefs are:

1. I can't disappoint others; I'm responsible for their well-being and happiness.

10

2. Others expect me to do what they want (whatever it is).
3. Life is interesting.

The unconscious goal of this style is to stay connected with that other person, no matter what.

The Control Type.

You're probably a Control personality if structure and organization are your top priority. You like competition; you like to win. You're assertive. You're law-abiding; you follow the rules. You like to get things done; you strive to be productive. You like to give orders. You're often in a leadership or management role. You thrive on order and predictability. These are some of your positive qualities.

Here are some of your negatives. You don't trust relationships because you don't trust people. You can be aloof and distant. You can be aggressive and even abusive if you feel threatened or challenged. You intensely dislike surprises or change. Because change is difficult for you, you avoid it. You're not flexible; you like your circumstances to remain constant. When life goes as planned, you're calm. When it doesn't, your anxiety builds. Then, you feel out-of-control, which is the very thing you work so hard to avoid.

A few of your core beliefs are:

1. I can control myself, the situation I'm in, and/or others to get the result I want or need.
2. Others can't be trusted; I can't depend on them.
3. The world is an unfriendly, unpredictable place.

If you're a Control person, you use your behavior to: (1) control yourself, or (2) control the situation you're in, or (3) control others. You can use each of these qualities alone or in any combination with each other.

The unconscious goal of this person is to feel emotionally, intellectually, socially, and physically safe all the time, no matter what.

11

1. Control Over Self.

If you're a person whose first goal is to control yourself, you don't share your feelings or thoughts, even if you know them. You are often silent; your actions may be minimal ones.

Core belief.

I'm not emotionally safe if I reveal myself.

2. Control Over Situations.

You control by taking charge of whatever situation you're in. You unconsciously reason that if you are in charge, you can prevent surprises. Surprises may mean change. If so, you no longer have control, which creates great anxiety, which pushes you to regain control, certainly assertively, maybe aggressively.

For example, you might consistently schedule each family member's social and work time the way you want it. You might organize your household's living space the way you want it. You might dominate the family checkbook, even when your partner protests. You do all of this because when you do, there will be no surprises. Being the leader in these areas promotes your feelings of calm and safety. Controlling people find it hard to "go with the flow" or to "wing it."

Core belief.

I feel safest when I'm in charge.

3. Control Over Others.

The shortest route to complete control is to control others. You do this by bossing, threatening, pushing or hitting. Maybe, you behave in these ways because you think you're right, and others shouldn't dispute you. Because you are correct, others should listen and do what you tell them to do.

Core belief.

I'm right.

4. Combinations of the Control Style.

Also, you might use some combination of these patterns. For example, heavy Self-Control ends up as passive Control of the Situation and of Others in it. That is, if you're silent, your quietness controls the situation and the people in it. Healthy relationship doesn't happen unless you connect, usually through talk.

And, if you control a situation, others in it will be controlled simply by being there. No one can change anything if you have a vise on it. In reverse, when you control people, you often control their situations, too.

Even though these combinations happen routinely, you have to look for them because they often happen subtly. Watch for passive Comfort and passive Control. They're the hardest to spot and the toughest to partner with.

The Superiority Type.

If you're a Superiority personality type, you love setting goals. You love achieving. You also love "to know." These are your top priorities. So, you constantly absorb information. Both knowing and achieving are integral parts of who you are. These promote the feeling of being on top of things, of being out in front. Why is "out in front" or "on top" so important? If you're not, your anxiety rises. To avoid this, you're always intensely busy doing something. These are some of your positives.

Here are some of your negatives. You're ALWAYS intensely busy doing something. You don't know how to relax, and you don't want to learn. Even when your body is resting, your mind is working. You not only have a daily "to do" list; that list has its own list. But, here's a drawback. Because you're constantly moving "forward" or "upward" toward some new place, you jeopardize your relationships. If you have to slow down or stop, you can get pretty irritated, anxious, or discouraged. Relationships don't do well with irritated, anxious, and discouraged.

13

Core Beliefs.

1. I must make a meaningful contribution in life.
2. Others shouldn't hold me back.
3. Life is full of interesting information, experiences, things to do, and places to go.

The unconscious goal of this style is to make progress, and, if possible, make it meaningfully, no matter what.

Summary.

Remember, all of these personality types are fluid. Beliefs may be owned by more than one style. So, look at each description as largely true, but not rigidly so.

We know that no one can be reduced to a description on a piece of paper. We're all too complex for that. Still, these descriptions are enormously helpful, if you use them to learn about you and others. Just remember not to use them to judge yourself or anyone else because of what you know.

ào ào ào

I'm sure you're getting to know yourself better. This is good.

ào ào ào

Memory Lane.

So, how do these beliefs form? The memories that follow: mine, Shannon's, and Erika's are all good examples.

Joan's Early Memories.

When I was three years old, my mother, father and I lived in a small apartment next door to a movie theatre. As little as I was, I would go out of the apartment to "go see the movies."

14

I remember feeling eager to go, and once I got there, feeling warm and comfortable. I have these same feelings today when I go to the movies.

My mother panicked the first couple of times I left the apartment. But, after finding me at the movie theatre, she and the usher agreed that I could "go to the movie" whenever I wanted. Since those were the days of the safe, neighborhood theatres, this worked out pretty well.

Looking at my behavior in the memory, I see that by three years old, I had already come to some unconscious conclusions: (1) about myself: how I should behave, (2) about others: how other people should treat me, and how they would behave with each other, and (3) about the world: what it was like, safe or dangerous.

Did I understand at three years old or twenty-five or even later, that I had formed a group of beliefs which directed my behavior? No, not at all. As an adult, if someone asked me why I went to the movies often, I replied that, "I just enjoy them." I knew nothing about belief systems. And, I wasn't aware that there was anything happening inside me during those pleasant afternoons. I was just enjoying the movies.

But, there was something going on. My personality style was forming continuously in those early years, just as yours was in you.

What personality types did I develop? Let's look at the memory I just reported. My beliefs fall mostly in the Superiority style because they go toward accomplishing goals: making my own decisions, taking risks, acting independently. Some of my beliefs are: (1) I'm curious; I should explore, (2) others should not slow me down, (3) the world is a pleasurable place to be.

❧❧❧

The next couple of memories illustrate why I developed my Pleasing type. Even though the content of these memories is different, the process I use in both is exactly the same. I'm about four years old. And, of course, these are only two of many others like them.

15

In one, I'm with my father at a horse stable. He tells me that we're going riding together. He smiles at me, and I feel so much love for him. I want very much to please him. So, even though the horse looks huge, and I feel scared about riding, I don't hesitate to do what my father expects me to do. I did ride the horse that day, and I felt so good because I did what my dad wanted.

In this next memory, even though the situation was different, my behavioral process was identical. In this one, I'm at a dance hall with both my mom and dad, watching them ballroom dance. (Later, I learned that when I was little, they entered quite a few ballroom dance contests and often won.) That night I'm happy just being there and watching them.

Then, to my surprise, my dad comes off the floor and asks me to dance. Everybody around the table is smiling and urging me to try. Between my dad and mom's coaxing and my wanting so much to please my father, my eagerness spills over. I go onto the floor to dance with him. I twirl and twirl. What fun! As young as I was, my dad taught me to dance, and all these years later, I still love it.

I formed some beliefs from these incidents and others like them: (1) I can't disappoint those I love, (2) others expect me to take care of their feelings, (3) the world is an exciting place. These are all Pleasing beliefs. Mostly, they are concerned with staying connected to that other person. And, the last one shows flexibility, which is a trait that all Pleasing people own.

ৰ৵ ৰ৵ ৰ৵

Now, Will You Try?

You see that when I look at my feelings and my behavior in these memories, I discover some of my beliefs. Why is this important? Your beliefs direct your behavior. To consciously direct your actions, you must uncover those beliefs. And, if you want to, and really try, you will, gradually.

16

Now, try to recall some of your early memories. Those before seven or eight years old are best. Once you've recalled what happened, ask yourself what your feelings were. Sometimes those are the most vital piece of the memory. Then, ask yourself what your motive was for behaving as you did in the memory. In your motives, you'll find your beliefs.

The memories that you recall and study should be "photo shot" images. Don't use your family's ritual events, like "Every Christmas our family did . . ." No. The ones you want are the one-moment-in-time, one-of-a-kind memories.

If you do this process, you'll recall some important happenings, and then gradually, you'll figure out your beliefs. Don't worry; with practice, you'll get on to it.

෬෬෬

More Instances.

Shannon and Erika discovered some beliefs from their early memories, just as I did from mine.

Shannon's Early Memories.

Shannon, his mother, father, and younger sister were eating their usual Sunday dinner together. Shannon was resisting eating some kind of vegetable when Tony, his uncle, came into the house and joined the family at the dinner table.

When Tony saw that Shannon wouldn't obey his mother, he grabbed the boy's arm and pulled him from his seat. Tony carried Shannon out of the dining room, and up the stairs into his bedroom. Leaving the door open so all could hear, Tony spanked him, and then left the boy in his room.

Time seemed to crawl by; Shannon felt scared and alone. After awhile, he crept to the top of the stairs where he could hear people talking. He hoped someone would come to

17

get him, but no one did. Later, he called for his mom but she didn't answer. He cried himself to sleep lying on the stairs. He was four years old.

Shannon formed mainly Superiority beliefs from this incident: (1) I'm alone in the world; I must take care of myself, (2) Others can't be counted on, (3) The world may be safer than my family.

Today, Shannon owns three small businesses. He's been financially independent, and away from his hometown since he turned 18 years old. He is living out his four-year-old convictions. Not only has he relied solely on himself and not on his family, but he's also very much a risk taker, who has succeeded on his own in his adult world. While he remains in touch with his original family members, he is not close to any of them.

Erika's Early Memories.

Erika reported three early "snapshot" recollections. In all of these, she used the same process, even though the situations, (the content), were different.

She was four years old when this incident occurred. "My mother and I had a huge, screaming fight on the way to church because I wanted to wear my black patent leather shoes even though it was raining. I remember sitting in the back seat while my mom shouted orders. I wondered: Why would she make me change shoes? I hate her. I want to wear what I want."

The second: "My mother insisted that I go to Sunday school. I didn't want to go. And, I refused to participate there. My teachers worried because they thought I didn't know how to use scissors; I was eight years old. I fooled them. That was how I paid them all back for making me do something I did not want to do."

The third: "In high school, I wanted to wear dress flats to school. My mother insisted I wear my saddle oxfords. I exploded inside and out. In the end, I sneaked my flats to school and changed at my locker. I won; I did what I wanted."

Erika felt her resentment grow every time her mother moved into what she thought was her own personal space. She felt intruded upon. By the time she reached sixteen, Erika keenly disliked her mother.

From these and other similar incidents, Erika formed Control of Self and Control of the Situation beliefs: (1) I'll do life the way I want, (2) Others shouldn't tell me, (3) When I'm out in the world, I'm freer.

After high school, Erika finished junior college and then took a receptionist position in a large corporation. When she left that company, l7 years later, she was successfully directing 45 people. Just as she had done 30 years before with her mother, she used her Control of Self and her Control Over the Situation beliefs to meet the demands of her job.

Like Shannon, today Erika is living out her long ago, unconsciously chosen beliefs.

る~る~る~

How Personality Formation Happens.

Remember, you developed your beliefs when you were very young. You decided on them by (1) imitating your parents, and also by (2) interacting with your parents and older siblings, if there were any.

Let's use the examples about Shannon, Erika, and me to illustrate this concept.

I adopted my Superiority behaviors by unconsciously watching and imitating my father. He was the eldest of eight children, and helped his mother parent his younger sisters and brothers. My dad died when I was young, but I still remember how he met life with tremendous energy and enthusiasm. He did whatever it took to take care of his family. As an adult, I did the same with my husband and children.

I developed my Pleasing beliefs because I loved my father, and I wanted him to be happy with me. Because I wanted

19

his love and approval, I, the inexperienced little girl, reasoned unconsciously that doing what he expected was how I could "fit in" with him. I concluded that if I pleased him, I would get the closeness I wanted. Later, I behaved in the same way with my husband and children.

Like mine, Shannon's Superiority developed because he imitated his dad. A fiercely independent man, Shannon's father had built a successful construction company by the time Shannon turned six years old. His father modeled his independence and strong work ethic until he died at age 72. Shannon, at 56, follows in his dad's footsteps.

Erika's styles developed for the same reason that Shannon's and mine did. Erika's mother's personality types were Control Over the Situation and Control Over Others. Erika's mother dominated the family's time and money, and all of its other resources. She managed Erika's father, Erika and Trish, her younger daughter, as tightly as she could. Erika hated being controlled but she saw the power in her mother's personality style, so she imitated it.

Erika remembers fighting her mother from two years old on, for control over herself, her space and her belongings. Once Erica left home at 19, she was in charge of not only her own space and schedule, but also, her husband's and daughter's. Her Control style, in its different forms, has kept her "in control" since then.

ॐॐॐ

More About Formation.

A child can watch one parent and take that parent's qualities almost completely. But, the child can also take characteristics from both parents. Shannon, Erika, and I are each the eldest child in our family systems. So, we had only adults to watch. If you have a different place in your family's birth order, you also had older siblings to interact with and to imitate.

If you're a first-born child, it's likely you took on the style of the parent you unconsciously thought was the stronger.

Maybe that parent was more verbal or initiated more action. So, he appeared to be the strongest. Your gravitation toward what you saw as strength was natural.

If you are a second-born, you probably took on the traits of the parent your older sibling did not choose. You did this for a couple of reasons. One, each child wants to carve out his own unique identity in the family system. He can't do that by imitating his older sibling, even when that child sets a good example. The second child won't compete with his older sibling in that sibling's space. He unconsciously reasons that he might fail to meet the older sibling's standard.

Two, when the older child chooses a parent, he takes up the "emotional space" around that parent. The second child doesn't believe that there is enough "emotional space" for him, too. So, he chooses the opposite parent to imitate because that space is uncontested.

This phenomenon partially explains why most first and second-born children behave so differently from each other. Remember, you made these unconscious decisions when you were very young because you had strong but unknown impulses that urged you to do so.

Who are you more like: mom or dad? Think of this broadly rather than specifically. In other words, you may not now behave exactly like your chosen parent, but you do behave generally more like him than your other parent.

If you are a third-born or later, your decisions about what to take from which parent are less clear and less predictable than those choices made by the first two children. So, you watched both parents as well as older siblings, and likely took qualities from all those above you.

Who are you more like: mom or dad or one of your older siblings?

Give all of these ideas more thought. The more you know about your beliefs and where they come from, the faster your awareness grows. That's what you want. Awareness equals inner strength.

21

One thing we know for certain; you clamped your infant antenna on a parent or sibling and molded yourself deliberately, but unknowingly, to that example.

ॐॐॐ

About You.

Two of the four personality types fits you more, the other two, less.

Gradually, make it your goal to recognize which beliefs you own. This will lead you to identify your personality type. You can start by doing the following.

◆ Think about which of the styles describe you best. Try to choose your top two types out of the four presented. (Try to identify your partner's top two types as well. Once you get familiar with your style, and how it's interacting with your partner's style, you'll feel relieved. Some of the mystery of your relationship starts to clear up.)

◆ If you are a first or second-born child, think about the traits you took from mom or dad. Think about how you and your next sibling are alike or different. Who is that sibling like?

◆ If you place later in your family, think about whom you imitated above you.

◆ Carefully observe your daily behavior. Then, ask yourself why you are doing what you are doing. The answers to your question will reveal your beliefs.

Then: (a) Watch your behavior to see where it is productive. Identify the beliefs that promote your good behavior. Keep those.

But: (b) Watch for behavior that is negative. Identify the beliefs that promote your bad behaviors. Those behaviors you will want to do something about quickly. Set a goal to stop them now.

22

♦ Use your early memories as Shannon, Erika and I did, to help you identify some of your beliefs. Remember, you can tell what your beliefs are by observing your behavior.

෭෨ ෭෨ ෭෨

Lastly, if you haven't identified your styles yet, don't worry. You'll find yourself in the deeper descriptions in Chapter Three.

෭෨ ෭෨ ෭෨

Applying Personality Type to Relationships.

You know already that you can use these personality concepts to help you understand yourself. Will the concepts also help you understand your partner? Can you use them to improve your relationship? Will they help you to live your life better everyday? And, then, can you bridge them over to the work and social areas of your life? Yes, to all of these questions, you can.

Here's an example of how one couple, Nancy and Ed, improved their relationship by understanding themselves, and each other, and by learning some talk skills. They had complained about repeating this same old destructive pattern over and over again. Frankly, both of them were really tired of it.

Ed and Nancy.

Several weeks before, Ed and Nancy had bought a security alarm for their home. On Sunday, Nancy realized that she had scheduled the installers for the next day. Since she and Ed hadn't decided where to put the alarm, Nancy asked him to come into the living room so they could choose a spot.

"Where do you think it should go?" Nancy asked. Ed indicated a place to the right of the door. She said, "Okay, I like that too, but let's see. Do you think maybe it would look better on the other side?" He immediately replied, "Do what you want!" and stalked out of the room.

23

When I asked her what her feelings were, she took a while to answer. Finally, she replied that they were a mixture of surprise, hurt, and then, anger. She was surprised and hurt because Ed's sharpness was unexpected. She was angry because, darn it, all she wanted was to have a discussion, and he disappeared. He "left" often.

I asked Ed what he thought about the incident. He said that he couldn't see much wrong with it, although he knew that he had upset Nancy. He admitted that this sort of thing occurred often. And, he said, he would probably keep "leaving;" he just wasn't going to argue with her.

Imagine you are Nancy. Your partner is Ed. You're trying to come to a decision with him. But, he won't talk about it. At first, you feel puzzled; you don't get it. But, as time goes on, you grow angry and tired of it. You wonder what in the world is going on. After all, these kinds of simple situations come up in marriage everyday. Why this trouble with them?

Imagine you are Ed. Your partner is Nancy. You wonder: what in the world is going on? After all, Nancy has strong opinions about everything. She knows what she wants. Why doesn't she just do it (whatever it is) and get it over with? Why is she bothering you? You don't care where the alarm goes.

If you're Nancy, you feel your respect for Ed dwindling, and your anger toward him rising. If you're Ed, you feel pressured by Nancy, and you resent her, sometimes bitterly, for it. Neither of you know how to fix it.

Now, if you keep the four personality styles in mind, you'll figure this situation out. You see that Nancy is a Superiority type; she sets goals, makes decisions, and moves forward. She also expresses herself well. She's an eldest child who grew up with a verbally strong father. She imitated him. So, she's comfortable with talk; she welcomes any discussion that will solve a problem, whatever that is. She saw her attempt to talk with Ed as an ordinary one.

Ed is also an eldest child. He, too, had a verbally strong parent: his mother. But, instead of imitating her, he grew up afraid of her. Because of his fear, he submitted to his mother's control. He imitated his father, who was passive. Ed decided to do whatever his mother wanted, just as his dad did. He learned to be quiet, and "go along," doing what he was told. When he went along in his childhood home, he kept himself pretty comfortable because he made his mother happy. For Ed, being comfortable was essential. This is the Comfort style.

Now, with the home alarm situation, he was just doing what he had done for the 38 years before he married Nancy: trying to stay comfortable. For him, that meant doing what Nancy wanted. He wouldn't risk a quarrel with her by giving his opinion. He kept quiet because he wanted to avoid conflict, no matter what it cost him. As you can tell, Ed had an awful fear of confrontation.

As a little guy, he decided that he would wait to be told "whatever." He knew that he should let mom and other adults make the decisions. Then, they would tell him what they wanted him to do. He knew not to bring up topics that might irritate anyone. So, as an adult, how did he handle his home and relationship responsibilities? He left them to Nancy. This makes sense, given his childhood.

Nancy, on the other hand, was an active, extra-responsible person. She couldn't just let issues float by without discussion and resolution.

Nancy saw relationship as a partnership. So, she tried to involve Ed. But, wait a minute. Ed didn't see relationship as a partnership. Passive styles don't expect to be partners; they expect to be told what to do, or they expect to be served or both. To be honest, Ed really didn't know how to partner. He was used to sitting back. Now, Nancy wanted him to join in when he didn't want to. Then, when Nancy kept after him, it really felt awful.

She, not realizing any of this, continued trying to involve Ed in their everyday life. She pursued him, to inform him ("nagged him," he said). As she pursued, he backed up. The more he backed up, the more she persisted. She hated the pattern because she felt bossy, like his mom. But, she also felt helpless. Sometimes, she almost hated herself for the way she

25

behaved. But, part of her thought he deserved to be pushed, even harassed. After all, he silently shoved her into a parent role when he refused to act. When she didn't pursue, he didn't involve himself.

Their exchanges ended with her feeling rejected and lonely. She really had a hard time respecting Ed.

On his side, Ed felt hounded and controlled, like he had always been with his mother. Ed loved Nancy, but at times, his anger equaled his love.

Each resented the other. The marriage worsened day by day.

As you can tell, they were both acting out beliefs that they had built years ago, unconsciously. But, their relationship wasn't working. And, until they understood themselves and each other better, they couldn't see why. Of course, the answer is that they have different, actually opposite, personality styles.

๛๛๛

Comment.

Probably any significant dissonance between you and your partner comes from differences in your personalities. But, problems come up for other reasons, too. (1) You are each complex. If you do not respect that complexity, you can create problems. (2) You may have some pure "communication" problems. Maybe, how you're stringing your words together isn't good. (3) Also, when your defenses argue with your partner's defenses, good relationship can't happen; you each close up. (4) And, when you and your partner own different values, conflicts occur. But, by far, wide differences in personality types cause the most serious relationship problems.

๛๛๛

Summary.

Here's what you know so far. You know that your beliefs direct your behavior. When you wish to change your actions, you know you must do so by changing your beliefs. Unfortunately, you can't make your behavior permanently different until you know the root, the belief it comes out of. So, you must discover the old roots, take them out, and plant new beliefs.

When Ed and Nancy understood that old beliefs caused their current destructive behavior, they chose to build new ones. Gradually, their new beliefs directed healthier behavior. Then later, as new everyday incidents arose, they handled them much better.

Ed learned to focus his attention. Instead of letting his mind or his body leave, he learned to stay and to participate, gradually. It wasn't easy for him to develop the inner discipline he needed. His first impulse was to run from relationship responsibility. After all, his need for comfort was very strong. But, gradually, he learned. Little by little, he chose healthier responses. And, as he did, his personal power grew. Slowly, he discovered that he liked being more equal with Nancy.

Realizing how even the thought of confrontation frightened Ed, Nancy promised him that there wouldn't be any conflict. There might be differences but they could be worked out calmly. Gradually, her reassurance encouraged him to stay and participate. Nancy valued Ed's opinions. His ideas were what she wanted from him, not a fight.

From her stronger position, Nancy learned not to startle him (ambush him, he said). She knew she could easily overwhelm him. Instead, she saw that when she wanted his opinion, it was best to warn him that a decision was coming up. Would he please think about it? That way, when it actually came time to talk, he came prepared.

She gave up her belief that things had to be settled right now. She "watered down" her intensity. She saw that Ed's rhythm of thinking and deciding differed from hers. It was slower, more laid back. She recognized that his calmness was a positive thing for her and their relationship.

Because they loved each other and they both valued the marriage, they each sacrificed some of their individual beliefs

27

and habits. They made the partnership their goal. And, they built new beliefs that supported it. Beliefs like:

1. Each partner pursues his own personality balance and brings it to the relationship.
2. Partners continually offer each other respect.
3. Partners are physically, emotionally, and verbally present to themselves and each other.
4. Partners commit to build friendship with each other.
5. Partners commit to listen, to participate, and to cooperate to find solutions.
6. Partners believe in compromise and work to reach it.

As Ed and Nancy grew more awareness, they enjoyed the closeness that healthy, smart relationships offer. Soon, they were really on their way. You can be, too.

ॐ   ॐ   ॐ

Big Ideas From Chapter Two.

1. *Personalities form by five years old. As a child, your goal was to fit in and belong. The personality you formed speaks for how you saw (and, now see) that you should do life.*

2. *We'll study four broad types:*

   Comfort
   Pleasing
   Control (3 versions)
   Superiority

3. *Use early memories to help identify your belief system.*

4. *Understand that you chose to be who you are because of your parent's example and your interactions with them.*

5. *Opposite personalities attract. This can be good because you complement each other. But, when the oppositeness is exaggerated, partnering may be difficult.*

6. *All can be worked out if you each make a goal of inner awareness and healthy communication, and pursue them together.*

7. *You each have the internal power you need to create a good relationship and a good life. You just need the skills to help you. Many of them are here in this book.*

Jump In;
Get To Know Yourself.

The heart has eyes which the brain
knows nothing of.

ક્ર   ક્ર   ક્ર

Chapter Three

Personality Types

A Deeper Look

*Y*ou've probably identified your personality types by now. But, if not, I'm sure you'll find yourself in the descriptions that follow. In this chapter, we'll explore nine factors that will help you get to know yourself. Looking at you like this can be fascinating; so, let's do it.

Remember, not every term in any one style will describe you, so you won't match any sketch exactly. It's impossible to completely capture you in these general descriptions; you're wonderfully incomparable. But still, this approach offers good accuracy. It's also speedy; you can get an idea of where you are quickly. For these reasons, it's a strong starting place for understanding yourself better.

Remember to look for two heavy and two less important personality types in your behavior. Although you use all four types every day, you lean heavily on two major ones.

It's common to use one of your main styles in intimate relationships. Your other style preference you use at your workplace.

For example, remember that Shannon owned three businesses. And, he used his Superiority to constantly move forward in his work to open new companies or expand the ones he had. But, in his intimate relationships with his wife and three children, he was very much the Pleasing style. And, Ericka owned the Control of the Situation style, which she'd learned from her mother. She used that style at work and at home. But, at home, she coupled that with a high Pleasing style. She provided her husband and daughter with lots of service. So, you see, you can mix them wherever you are.

1. Temperament.

Here we're looking at your qualities, your disposition, your personality. The following traits show up consistently in your everyday living.

Which two of these descriptions fit you best?

The Comfort Type.

If you're the Comfort type, the things you love most are those that make you feel good. You especially want physical and emotional comfort, but you also want every other part of your life to be easy. You're laid-back, mellow; you're easy to get along with. You like to entertain and be entertained; you love fun. You are often sentimental, even romantic. You make few demands on others. You avoid other's expectations; they create too much pressure. You live for "now" and don't plan for tomorrow. You mind your own business; you avoid conflict. Your behavior is predictable. If this description fits you, one of your personality types is Comfort.

The Pleasing Type.

If you're the Pleasing type, making others feel good, especially those you care about, is what you love the most. You hate to disappoint people; so you're willing to do whatever they expect, reasonable or not. You feel responsible for getting whatever needs doing, done. So, you're flexible enough to change plans at a moment's notice to accommodate someone else's needs. For the same reason, you're likely to volunteer

32

when something needs doing. You're friendly and considerate. You're a sympathetic person. You're cooperative, not competitive. You're anxious to compromise and good at doing it. If most of these qualities belong to you, it's likely that one of your personality types is Pleasing.

The Control Type.

If you're the Controlling type, the thing you love the most is order and structure. It's predictable. So, you are organized. You're a detail person. Being productive is important to you and so you persist in getting things done. You're assertive, directive and even aggressive when you decide to be. You like competition because you like to win. You're law-abiding. You're conscientious about following rules; you expect others to be the same. You have strong leadership skills; you often lead the way in speaking out about issues. If these traits are yours, you're a Control style.

You use your control in one of three ways, or in any combination of them: Control of Self, Control of the Situation, and/or Control of Others.

If you are a Control of Self person, you control your own behavior instead of controlling others. You act and speak minimally and quietly. If you are a Control of the Situation person, you use your qualities to shape the setting you're in. That place may be your home, your workplace, or elsewhere. If you are a Control of Others person, you use your qualities to directly dominate people.

You may use more than one of these control approaches at the same time. It might not be unusual for you to control yourself and the situation you're in, but not others. Or, maybe you show no ability to control yourself, but you attempt to control others and the setting you're in.

Even if you do use more than one type of Control, you still have another strong style. It's rare to see a person with only Control types operating.

33

For example, a style combination that I see often is Control of Self or Control Over the Situation along with Pleasing. (This is the best combination for parenting that I've seen. The Control sets the authority and the boundaries for the child and the Pleasing provides what the child needs.) Another combination that's common is Superiority and Control over Others. Not much softness there.

One duo that I see infrequently is Superiority and Comfort. The person who owns this combination has a hard time with himself. He's driven to set and achieve goals at the same time he wants an easy life. That's tough.

The Superiority Type.

If you're the Superiority type, the thing you love the most is "to know." Because you love information, you're well informed. You may be an expert about one or more subjects. Not only do you like to gather information, you also like to share it (instruct), use it (write about it), talk about it (many hours of discussion), and so forth.

You're consistently working on a wide variety of goals, from short-term to long-term. You like to be precise; so you're thorough in everything you do. You may even want to do it (whatever it is) perfectly. You hold yourself and others to very high standards, although those measures seem ordinary to you. You're industrious and persistent, so you produce more than others expect. The quantities seem normal to you.

You are idealistic with strong moral and ethical values. You believe in social justice; you probably believe that you must take care of less fortunate people. If this description fits you, chances are you're a Superiority person.

෮෮෮

Tune In.

Now, about your partner's personality styles, start tuning into your feelings when you are together. If you're having fun or taking it easy most of the time, your partner is probably Comfort. If you feel taken care of, he's probably Pleasing.   If you feel challenged or he seems remote, he's probably Control.   If you greatly admire him, or if you feel less adequate than him, he's probably Superiority.

If you don't know how you feel when you are together, take more time to study him. Gradually, if you're observing both him and yourself carefully, you'll be able to decide which qualities and behaviors describe him best. Then, be aware of the feelings generated in you when you're together.

ର୍ଚ୍ଚ ର୍ଚ୍ଚ ର୍ଚ୍ଚ

2. Unknown Motive; What Is Your Purpose?

All behavior has purpose behind it (if only habit), even if the behavior looks casual. Actions do not happen randomly.

Remember, long ago you decided how you would fit in and belong. Now, you do what you do because of those early decisions, even though those may be unknown to you. As you observe you, ask yourself what motives drive your actions. Ask yourself why you do what you do.

Remember, to get good information, you must be curious about you. You must observe yourself, and then ask you what those observations turn up. As you do, be patient with yourself and the process. If you persist, you'll realize a rewarding payoff.

Here are more clues that should help identify possible motive. Which two types are yours?

The Comfort Type.

Is your primary motive in life to experience pleasure and comfort? If so, you're the Comfort type.

The Pleasing Type.

Is your primary motive a deep bond with others? One of your styles is Pleasing.

The Control Type.

Is your primary motive to heavily direct/control yourself, your setting and/or the people in your life? You're Control.

The Superiority Type.

Is your primary motive to complete meaningful goals that move you forward? The Superiority style does that.

❧❧❧

Your Partner?

Now, about your partner, study him as intensely as you study yourself. Think about what you observe. If you can, draw some conclusions. Ask him if they are correct. Then, invite him to do the same with you.

❧❧❧

3. Retreats From; Avoids.

When you, the child, decided on your beliefs, you unconsciously adopted what made you FEEL the best. You avoided people and situations that made you FEEL bad. Of course, you were not consciously aware that you were doing this.

Now you, the adult, may exaggerate your behavior because you want to avoid these feelings. Why is the avoiding so important to you? Experiencing these feelings, whatever they are, creates in you another more desperate feeling: anxiety. You don't think you can handle it. As you read on, notice that each personality type fears and, therefore, avoids a different feeling.

The Comfort Type (avoids Stress, Pressure.)

You want to avoid feeling stressed, pressured or responsible to others. You resist expectations; they create anxiety. Anxiety creates major discomfort. Discomfort goes against your core beliefs.

Claudia is a stay-at-home mom. She has three sons, ages 15,13 and 10. They all play sports so all three have heavy practice and game schedules through the year. Claudia wants her sons to be involved. And, she loves socializing with other parents; she has a great time.

But, the good moments don't make up for the discomfort and pressure she feels at other times. For example, she hates driving in bad weather to games that go on at all hours of the day and night. The traveling to tournaments, the unfamiliar hotels, the long hours seem to her like they're designed just to annoy her. By any sport's midseason, she's anxious beyond reason because she feels so pressured. At that point, her husband takes over, even though he works 60 hours a week. He doesn't have a choice; she isn't going to do it. She's too stressed and uncomfortable.

The Pleasing Type (avoids Rejection).

You want to avoid feeling rejected. So, you unconsciously reason that if you do what others expect, certainly with those you love, but others too, you won't disappoint them. If you don't disappoint them, they won't reject you. Even anticipating emotional distance, never mind a real breach between you and that other person, makes you anxious.

Toni, Lisa's daughter, wants some new clothes. Lisa's answer was, "No," the first time Toni asked. And, for good reasons: One, Toni has plenty of nice clothes to wear; two, she is manipulating Lisa and Lisa knows it. But, she does buy the clothes. Toni is so good at cold, silent withdrawal that Lisa

37

CAN'T STAND IT.   She can't bear the anxiety she feels during the emotional separation from Toni. And, Toni counts on that.

The Control Type (avoids Surprise and Embarrassment).

You want to avoid feeling embarrassed, surprised or humiliated.   Anticipating these feelings makes you acutely anxious. So, you unconsciously reason that you won't feel these awful feelings if you control yourself, your setting, other people or all of it.

Control Over Self.

Emma is the youngest of five children.   At 36 years old, Emma still can't say what she really thinks about anything to her mother or her four older siblings. She dreads the criticism she's so used to getting from them.   All the time she was growing up, her brother and sister, Tommy and Alexis, made fun of her every single day.   Emma reasoned unconsciously, that they would stop if she stopped. So, she did; she just stopped talking.

Rationally, this makes no sense at all. But, Emma isn't thinking rationally.   She's reacting to the awful feelings that caused so much pain long ago.

Control Over the Environment.

Tom came from a poor family. In school, kids insulted him daily about his old, patched clothing or his ragged school bag.   Tom decided that when he grew up, he would keep everything he owned in tip-top shape. Then, he could feel pride, not humiliation, ever again.

Now, Tom's wife, Lydia, can't carry a cup of tea from one room to the next without Tom warning her, "Don't spill it; you'll stain the carpet." Tom worries about keeping his appliances in good shape.   So, he supervises the use of the washer and dryer and the refrigerator and the microwave, the stove and the oven. Oh yes, and the dishwasher, too. Tom won't let Lydia or their two teen daughters use the CD player; after all, it's expensive equipment. Keeping all of these possessions in tiptop shape means, symbolically, that he's okay.

By controlling his environment tightly, Tom thinks that he's making sure he'll never feel humiliated again.

Control Over Others.

You think that the best way to eliminate surprises or prevent change is to control others. Because people have ideas, wants and needs that don't always coincide with yours, you can't predict how they will act. If you can't predict what is coming up, you must deal with surprises and changes. But, you believe you can't. Both of these make you feel too ANXIOUS.

For a family reunion, Al and his brothers and sisters were going to a major league baseball game. Al assumed that Joy, his wife, would go with him. After all, she always did whatever he wanted. Joy, though, at 56 years old, was practicing becoming her own person. She told him nicely, that she didn't want to go; she really wasn't that interested in baseball.

This was a mighty surprise for Al and an unpleasant one at that. And, the only way he knew to deal with this situation was to bully her into going. After all, he believed that husband and wife should do things together and his thoughts were always correct. Furthermore, she had always done what he asked/told her to. Never mind what Joy wanted; she was just being selfish.

The Superiority Type (avoids Meaninglessness).

You, the child, believed that you had little value or meaning in your family. This belief created too much pain and anxiety for you. So, you compensated. You discovered that when you set goals and reached them, you felt solid and substantial. So, you got busy "doing".

As Bill was growing up, his parents told him that they hadn't planned to have so many children (he was the fifth child of six). The implication was that he was an unwanted burden. To

39

make it worse, his dad told him over and over that he was stupid and would never amount to anything.

So, from first grade on into high school, Bill made trouble at home and at school; he was nearly uncontrollable most of the time. Nobody at his high school thought he could make it through. Of course, it was a given; he would drop out.

But, in his junior year, Bill broke out of his emotional swamp. He graduated from high school, worked for six months, and then enrolled in a course for paramedics. He did well with this career, which lasted about five years. But, he wanted more.

He created more. He acquired the necessary credentials to become a Physician's Assistant. Working as a valued partner with eight pediatric neurologists for the past fifteen years, he feels wonderful. His contributions to his team have brought Bill high esteem and a good living. Along the way, he's acquired his Master's Degree in Business. And, recently, he took on new and challenging work in the psychiatric division of a renowned hospital.

This is pretty good for the little kid whose parents told him that he was worthless and would never accomplish anything. Half of him confronts his deceased parents, "See, you never knew me or loved me; too bad for you." The other half of him mourns, "Father and mother, why did you never know me? I tried so hard to fit in so you would love me."

卷卷卷

Don't Worry; You'll See It.

You probably know your styles by now, but if you're still uncertain, study the people you know. Sometimes, it's easier to identify other's personality types than it is your own, particularly when you're new at this process.

As you observe, ask yourself why different people adopted their styles. What does he avoid? What could be the motive behind her actions? What is he trying to achieve with his behavior?   Why does she wait rather than act?   Then, ask yourself these same questions.   I'll bet you turn up some provocative answers. Our behaviors are so interesting.

෪෪෪

4. Common Personality Type Beliefs.

Each type owns beliefs that are common to it.   The lists below aren't complete, but they give some of the CORE beliefs for each style.   In your two types you probably own many of those listed.   You use them consistently, although until now, maybe unconsciously.

Three things to remember: One, you shaped your belief system by age four or five.   Because you were a keen observer, you forged many correct beliefs.   But, you also formed some wrong conclusions because you were young and inexperienced.

Two, your beliefs explain (a) your view of how you will "fit in" in your family.   They also tell what (b) you believe about how others should treat you.   And, they reveal how (c) you view the outside world.

Three, your family home had it's own rituals, values and mottos.   It had its one-of-a-kind atmosphere.   You either absorbed or rejected what was there.

But, the real world is not your original family. The world has its own atmosphere, its own culture and customs, its own demands, and so on. So when you, now grownup, try to live out the beliefs you formed long ago, some of them won't work. It's these unproductive, unbalanced beliefs that we study here. Keep in mind that even good beliefs often "turn bad" when you exaggerate them.

Now, if you want to be healthy and have a happy, successful life, you must be positive and balanced. Then, you'll handle your adult relationships and situations well.   Being healthy means giving up any exaggerated form of the beliefs listed below.

41

శ్రీశ్రీశ్రీ

If learning about yourself seems like a big job, try not to be discouraged; you can do it. The only hard thing about altering your beliefs is finding out what they are. When you know your beliefs, you'll take charge of them. I trust you with this; you should trust you, too.

శ్రీశ్రీశ్రీ

Some Core Comfort Beliefs.

Life must be easy.
Life must be comfortable; it must feel good.
I don't deal with the world's reality; it's uncomfortable.
I can make up my own reality.
I can do life any way I want.
I don't have to be responsible for myself emotionally (and,
  sometimes, not physically, socially or financially either).
Others will do it (whatever it is) for me.
Others shouldn't ask me for anything.
If others ask, my first response will be "No;" I'm uncomfortable
  with expectations.
I don't need to say "I'm sorry" for whatever goes wrong, even if I
  am at fault.
I can't stand pressure, stress or expectations.
I don't have to listen.

Some Core Pleasing Beliefs.

I should be vigilantly responsible.
I should feel sorry for others.
I should not disappoint others.
I should take care of others.
I need someone to love, someone to be connected with.
I should always be available for those I care about.
My first response to requests will be "Yes."
I can't stand rejection.
I shouldn't ask for anything, when I focus on me, I'm being
  selfish.
My needs and wants come last.

I must listen extremely well so that I always know what others need.

Some Core Control Beliefs.

I'm right (about whatever).
It's my responsibility to tell others what to do and how to do it.
Others should listen to me.
I should control myself, my situation and/or other people to get the result I want.
I can't stand to feel humiliated.
I can't stand change; it interrupts my control.
I can't stand surprises; they scare me.
I must be in charge.
I can't trust others.
I'm suspicious of intimate relationships because I don't trust.
I don't need to say I'm sorry for whatever goes wrong, even if I am at fault.
My first response to requests will be "No."
I don't have to listen; I already know.

Some Core Superiority Beliefs.

I know (whatever) because I love information.
I must make some meaningful contribution to life.
I should treat life seriously.
I should be responsible.
I should always do the right thing.
I should be curious.
I can't do anything halfway; it must be done thoroughly.
I should be precise, accurate and maintain high standards and so should others.
I can do it all, that is, all of my goals.
My first response to requests can be "Yes" or "No."
I can't wait or slow down; I'm too busy; I'm in a hurry.
I don't have time to listen.

You might wonder: could some, but not all of these beliefs describe me? Yes, absolutely. But, chances are high that in your type, you'd own most of the beliefs on these lists, if not all.

You might also wonder if these are the only beliefs for your type. No, no. Of course, you'd also own many other healthy ones. But, we don't worry about or study those here because they already work for you. So, they're not a concern.

The ones listed above don't "work" for you, especially when you exaggerate them. Instead, they cause you trouble. If you learn about them, you can drop or amend the ones you don't like. You can even keep unhealthy beliefs. But, if keeping them is what you choose, you should at least take charge of them, instead of them directing you. When you are unaware of your beliefs, they're in charge of you because they program your behavior automatically, but unconsciously.

By choosing awareness, you live smarter. And, certainly, that's what you want.

❧ ❧ ❧

5. Your Parent's Role in your Formation.

Often in session, I'll identify someone's behavior as Pleasing or Control or one of the other styles. My client and I talk further about who used this behavior most in their original family, mom or dad? My client will usually say something like: "Oh yeah, that's like my dad," or "I didn't realize it but I must have gotten that from my mom." Yes, you did. And I did, too, take my qualities from both of my parents. In fact, the belief system that you and I created unconsciously developed directly from one or both of our parents' lifestyles. We imitated them, not knowing, of course, that we were doing it.

It's helpful if you identify the types your parents used in their own lives. Because they used them with each other, with you and with your siblings, you lived with them every day. If you can recognize some of your parent's behavior patterns, you'll be more likely to understand why you developed as you did.

As a child you absorbed what you saw being acted out. As an adult, you use it.

Understanding the root of your behavior helps you in several ways. First, if you decide that you want to change a behavior, you'll be more successful if you know its origin.

Second, trying to change behavior without knowing where it comes from usually results in success for a short time, but not permanently. Understand; your original belief system is incredibly strong. It has a long track record of control over you. Because it's so powerful, it won't give up easily.

If you're dedicated to shifting your behavior, you'll need to remind yourself over and over that you are in charge of you. Your old belief system is not. Soon, if you don't already, you'll know why the beliefs are there; you'll know what behavior they direct and you'll know what you intend to change about them.

Third, let's say that your parents behaved in ways that you disliked. You knew their actions were wrong; they caused you pain. But, unconsciously, you adopted them. You'll be motivated now if you remind yourself of the pain and harm their actions caused you long ago. Maybe it even continues now. If you make the connection between what caused you pain and misery long ago and your parent's beliefs and behavior, you will strengthen your resolve to drop those behaviors.

Fourth, knowing the origin of some of your beliefs will give you a grounded feeling, a sense of calm. It's a closure on any confusion or mystery you may have felt about why you're behaving as you do. Knowing yourself is not only a good thing; knowing yourself is a powerful tool.

≈≈≈

Now, about your partner: you might ask him to do this same process with his original family history. You will both understand him better if you can identify the parental behaviors that influenced his development. As you understand each other better, it helps your relationship.

≈≈≈

Parent's Types.

Remember, you can "catch" your style either by: (1) watching it displayed by a parent and then imitating it, or by (2)

45

interacting with your parents. I'll explain what I mean. Then, you'll want to think about how each of your parent's styles directly affected you.

The Comfort Type.

If your heaviest style is Comfort, you probably had a Comfort parent who owned that style and modeled it for you. In other words, you saw your parent acting out the Comfort beliefs mentioned above and enjoying the benefits. So, you decided to adopt the Comfort style because you liked the feelings it created and the rewards it provided.

On the other hand, you might own the Comfort style because of the interaction between you and your parent(s). This is what I mean. If one or both of your parents served you as Pleasing parents do, you probably concluded that you should sit down, get comfortable and let life happen. This is because you, the child, saw that "Someone else would do it." This is a core Comfort belief.

Or, if one or both of your parents controlled you, you would have concluded that you should stay out of the way so that you wouldn't get into trouble. This is how you, the child, got the message that "I don't have to be responsible." This is also a core Comfort belief.

Remember, you can "catch" a style in either of two ways. One is by imitating it; the child watches and copies the parent. The other is by being pleased, served or controlled by your parent(s).

Kathy.

Kathy is the oldest of five women siblings. Her father, a quiet man, worked hard and supported his family well. But, at home, after work and dinner, he sat down and watched television. He didn't have hobbies and he didn't actively participate in making decisions or originating ideas or action for his family. He passively waited for Kathy's mother to do it.

Kathy's mom, on the other hand, busied herself with running the household. Kathy watched her mother take care of her dad, her four younger siblings and her, too. Mom was the Pleasing type. Kathy concluded, unconsciously, that she liked being waited on; it felt pretty good. And so symbolically, she sat down like her dad and became a Comfort person.

Now, Kathy's married to John. Being over-responsible, John runs his own business, takes care of their household, Kathy and their children, too. His style is just like Kathy's mom's style; he's Pleasing. John indulges Kathy, just as her mother did.

Kathy developed her style by: (1) imitating, "unconsciously watching," her dad, and by (2) receiving service from her mom. She concluded that she would use passive behavior to fit in and "belong" in her family. In life, she would expect others to take care of her, to serve her.

Remember, you, as a child, developed beliefs in three life areas: (1) how you should behave to best "fit in" and "belong" in your family, (2) how you should expect others to treat you and each other, and (3) how you would "do" the outside world.

❧❧❧

The Pleasing Type.

If your heaviest style is Pleasing, you probably had a Pleasing parent who modeled that style for you. You imitated him because unconsciously you admired that parent; you wanted to be like him.

Or, you might have developed this style because a Controlling parent made you his target. This parent didn't treat you with respect. Even worse, your parent might have rejected you.

There are many levels of emotional rejection. Maybe your parent verbally or physically punished you. Or, maybe it was subtle, not apparent to siblings or others, but you felt it. Realizing this unconsciously, you might have tried harder to "fit

47

in" by pleasing your parent. You thought that if you did what he expected, you would be accepted, and given the love you so desperately wanted.

Jennifer.

Jennifer, an extremely capable 52-year-old woman, runs her own business. Her firm provides accounting services to small companies.

Jennifer developed her pleasing style by watching her parents. Her dad and mom both worked and they also shared responsibilities at home. While her brother above her "sat down" and received all the "waiting on," especially from her mother, Jennifer imitated both parents. She got a "double dose" example of responsibility and care-taking from both parents.

Now, she's married to her opposite style. David is a passive, timid man. Even at his work he's neither energetic nor assertive. Her husband is like her older brother. In one way or another, Jennifer has taken care of both her brother and husband nearly all of her life. Added to that personal service, she also runs her own business and her household and cares for their two young children.

We all agree that responsibility is an emotionally necessary trait. But, Jennifer is creating a potential physical disaster. Why? She's doing it all, all alone. Sooner or later, if there's no change, she'll break, probably with heavy fatigue or anxiety symptoms.

Did her parents plan this for Jennifer? No; but they both presented strength in many ways. Jennifer, being a strong child, decided that it was her job to take care of others. That's the Pleasing style.

ॐॐॐ

The Control Type.

If your heaviest style is Control, you probably had a Controlling parent who provided a strong example. Your parent acted out these beliefs: (1) Controlling myself, my situation and/or others keeps me "in charge" and helps me handle my anxiety, (2) I like giving orders, running things and moving people around; it helps me feel safe, (3) When I'm in charge, I don't have to deal with surprises or change. Power is usually attractive, even to children who do not consciously understand it.

But also, you might be the controlling style because you had a Pleasing parent who served you. Very often, a mother, especially, thinks that she is a good parent if she provides everything her child needs. So, she does. If one of your parents waited on you, you probably concluded that you were important and should get special treatment. Did your unsuspecting, devoted parent give you too much power?

ॐॐॐ

A Side note.

Pleasing parents often turn out a Controlling child, while Controlling parents often turn out a Pleasing or Comfort child. (Isn't this amazing? Earlier in my work, I thought it would be just the opposite.)

About the Pleasing child: As the child of a Controlling person, you might be afraid of your parent. It would make sense, then, if you unconsciously decided to be quiet and passive. It would make sense too, if you decided that you should be compliant and obey, rather than risk thinking and behaving independently. Thus, you developed your Pleasing style.

About the Controlling child: If you were this child, you would unconsciously conclude that you are more important than your parent, because your Pleasing parent serves you and neglects himself. Or, you might conclude, because of your parent's service, he intends you to have control in your relationship. Because of your inexperience, you, the child, wouldn't consciously think about whether this made sense or not. During this process, of course, the Pleasing parent doesn't see the power being shifted from him to you.

ॐॐॐ

Jeffrey.

Jeffrey, a second-born child, followed a Pleasing sister, Joyce. She took on the lifestyle of her mother. Since Joyce had taken his mother's traits, Jeffrey imitated his father, who used a Controlling style.

Jeffrey developed beliefs like his father's: (1) Life is a competition, (2) I need to stay in control or someone will control me, (3) I should always be on guard with people, (4) I'm right.

Jeffrey's father was a high-level business executive. Jeffrey saw his father always in charge: the boss. He saw his father's strength in decision-making, in initiating, following through and completing projects. Jeffrey saw his father's ability to control situations and other people. Jeffrey knew that what his father decided was important because others would do what he told them to do. He saw that his father had power and concluded that his dad could do whatever he wanted to.

Even though he was treated like a prince and could have developed into the Comfort style, Jeffrey was a strong child with an abundance of intense energy. So, we see that Jeffrey's Control style developed for two reasons: (1) his father's example and (2) his mother's and his sister's service.

Jeffrey's occupation today is similar to his father's back then. He has a Masters Degree in Business and works as a vice-president in a large corporation. He manages about twenty people. His first and most important style is Control.

Jeffrey has a family of his own now. In it he suffers from distance in each of his relationships, even though he loves his wife, Jan, and their two children. Jan loves her husband, too, but is lonely. No wonder. Jeffrey really hasn't learned how to reveal his feelings to himself or to Jan. He's unconsciously afraid of intimacy.

The Superiority Type.

If your heaviest style is Superiority, you probably had a Superiority parent who knew how to set and reach goals. That

50

parent constantly moved forward. The involvement and accomplishment you saw looked exciting to you. You adopted the style by imitating it.

On the other hand, you might have developed this style because you doubted your value in your family. Maybe you felt unimportant there. If so, you unconsciously decided that you must avoid feeling meaningless; for you, it's the worst feeling of all. It's worse than feeling powerless (Control), even worse than being rejected (Pleasing). It's far worse than being stressed (Comfort). You can handle any amount of stress, if you feel you have worth and your life means something.

It's also possible that your parents emphasized good and bad, right and wrong, success and failure, instead of emphasizing how you should develop yourself. Did your parents shame or humiliate you if you did not "do good" or if you weren't always right or if you were interested in different things than they were?

If you were shamed, you decided that you would reject the message that you have no value. You decided to do life so that you could feel valuable in it, even if you were not valued in your birth family. And so, you quickly went forward.

Alex.

Alex, the baby of six siblings, developed his Superiority style because: (1) his father's primary style is Superiority (his father provided the model), and (2) his father shamed and humiliated his older siblings; he didn't treat them with respect. From his child's perspective, Alex concluded that his father didn't value his older siblings. He certainly didn't want to repeat their experience.

Alex wanted to convince his parents that he did have value. So, unconsciously he reasoned that the best way to earn his father's respect was to achieve; this would make both of his parents proud of him. Then, he'd never be shamed or humiliated. His parents would indeed value him; he would have meaning in his life.

51

Obedient and cooperative, Alex progressed through high school with an "A" average. In his spare time, he became an accomplished, performing musician. Then, he went off to college.

Four years later, Alex graduated with a degree in criminal justice. With that in hand, he obtained a job in the state's Attorney General's office. He stayed there five years. Subsequently, he returned to college, this time to law school. Three years later and now an attorney, he took a position clerking for a circuit court judge. He has recently applied for a position with the Federal Bureau of Investigation. He's not sure if he'll be accepted but he knows that wherever he goes from here, it will be "forward" and "up."

Very much the Superiority style, Alex has beliefs like: (1) I can't waste time; I have to move ahead, (2) I can't stand feeling bored, (3) I love to "know" everything, (4) I must do everything to a high standard, (5) my work must have symbolic and lasting meaning.

෴෴෴

Let's Pause.

By now, you see that your parent's personalities were dramatically important in shaping your own. Their personalities along with your early exchanges with them, helped set your course for life. In those dialogues, what were your parent's attitudes toward you? Do you know what they thought of you? And, more important than the interactions between you, is how you felt about the exchanges. Your family was the first world you knew as a child. For a time, your family was your whole world. How you fit, or didn't fit into it shaped your personality. Your parent's reflection of who you were in the family was important. Was it positive or not? Think about it.

෴෴෴

Other Influences.

You've seen how your parent's styles affected you. But you, the child, had other factors to consider, too. You weighed these also, unconsciously, as you put together your whole lifestyle. Let's look at some of those other influences.

1. **Heredity and Genetics:** First, your body has its own unique DNA combination. So, you have a distinct physical composition that's only yours. Even though you started with your parent's genes, the mix of these makes you a new human being.

   Then, you had your own birth experience. Your birth was probably an ordinary one, as it is for most of us. So, you had nothing unusual to handle there.

   But, if you, or a sibling had an unusual physical condition at birth, or soon after, your belief system reflects that even now. Here's how.

A Family With Physical Disability.

   Some time back a family of six adult siblings, two men and four women, came in for help. The prior month, in August, all six of them, with their spouses and children, had gone on vacation together. During that week the youngest and the oldest sisters, Lisa and Norma, exchanged bitter words.

   All the siblings felt discouraged. Although there had been tension between these two women for a while, they hadn't been so direct or ugly with each other until the vacation. Their other siblings really didn't know what caused the arguments. And, they didn't know what to do about them.

   Actually, Lisa and Norma had resented each other for years. Most family members knew that. But now, their exchanges were becoming more brutal. How had they gotten to this point? After all, Lisa and Norma were sisters; they were supposed to love each other.

   This problem actually started 30 years ago, when Lisa was born with a defective heart valve. There were a few operations, and along with them, complications. Frightened, her parents hovered over her. And, they expected all of their other children to help create a no-stress atmosphere for Lisa. Her parents thought she needed that while she recuperated.

Of course, Lisa formed predictable beliefs given the service she received. Because her parents insisted that she rest while her brothers and sisters took care of things, this became a way of life for her. She believes she's "special." Because she's different, the others owe her special treatment. And, she believes she should be careful because, after all, she was very sick, and she could be again. Now, at 35, Lisa continues acting out these original ideas, in spite of this reality: her health has been good for the last 25 years.

Norma resents her youngest sister. Looking back, she took care of Lisa and her other four siblings the whole time she was growing up. And, this is the treatment she gets for it now? She feels set up by her parents and used by Lisa. She did all the work, but now Lisa gets the payoff in service and sympathy.

Norma's growing hostility scared Lisa; she didn't understand it. Norma's idea that Lisa should behave like the rest of them seemed a strange one to Lisa. After all, she had this serious condition. And, she had never acted like them. Why would she start now? Because of her problem, she believes that she's different from them, and should always be treated with more care. Lisa can't make any sense of Norma's feelings or thoughts.

The tension that had been in the atmosphere at every family gathering for the last few years had just peaked during their vacation together. The brothers and sisters all felt sorry for Lisa as they always had. Because Norma knew that, she could feel their collective disapproval when she confronted Lisa, even in small ways. Gradually, Norma withdrew; she didn't think she had a choice.

Back home from vacation now, the other siblings just wanted peace in the family. But, they didn't know how to make that happen. They felt helpless in the face of something they didn't understand, and couldn't change. And, each of them was uncertain what their roles with Lisa and Norma should be. The whole thing was pretty confusing for them.

The one thing they were each certain of, though, was that they loved each other and wanted everyone to get along again.

Little by little, we sorted out all six sets of individual beliefs. We looked at each sibling's role in the family group. Gradually, as they all saw how powerfully childhood beliefs direct behavior, they understood Lisa's and Norma's actions better. Each of them understood that they could choose more appropriate and healthy behavior. Each of them worked at improving their communication and negotiation skills with each other. Slowly, slowly each person alone, and all of the family members together began to heal.

I give this example so you can see how special health circumstances often make fundamental changes in a person's personality formation. When the young sibling's responded to their parent's concerns about Lisa's sickness, dynamics within the group changed forever.

Fortunately, most of us do not have unusual, physical conditions to deal with as we begin our lives.

෨෨෨෨

More Influences (continued).

Okay, mostly we've been discussing the belief system. Now, let's look at some other factors, too, that seriously influenced your entire lifestyle formation. Aside from your genetic makeup, there were your (1) birth order, (2) the atmosphere in your home, (3) the quality of the connection between you, and the other family members, and (4) your parent's values affected your formation choices. Let's look at these.

2. **Your Birth Order:** are you a first-born, second-born, third-born, or an only child? You formed your lifestyle watching

those above you. This includes not only your parents, but also any older siblings. What personality types do your siblings own? How did your siblings relate to you?

3. **The Atmosphere:** the mood of your home influenced you. Was the climate turbulent and chaotic, in crisis all of the time? Or, did you live with the opposite: silence? Was your home a biting, competitive place, or a softer one that emphasized cooperation and solving problems? Was fear or confidence the dominant feeling in your home? Were your parents frank and open with their feelings and thoughts, or were they closed?

4. **Emotional Connection:** were you "connected" to your family members? In other words, were your family members friendly? Did people engage each other? Did each person talk freely and safely? Did they generally trust each other? This is the healthy engaged family.

   Or, were your family members more aloof, cool? Did you each live more separate and parallel lives, and didn't share information? Did you respect each other? Did you trust each other? This system is more detached, but could still be a healthy one, if there were loving connections. Which description fits your original family?

5. **Values:** your parents valued certain behaviors and possessions and activities enough to spend their personal resources, that is, their time, money or energy on them.

   For example, maybe your parents enjoyed sports, music, camping, the theatre, or travel. If so, they exposed you to these activities as you grew up. And, maybe your parents acted out fairness and honesty every day. Whatever your parents stood for and valued, they exposed you consistently to that. Whatever their values were, you probably adopted them, and use them today.

   On the other hand, there's always a chance that you rebelled against your parents, and rejected what you saw was important to them. If that is true, your values today will be different than those of your parents, maybe even opposite their choices.

If you were a child who didn't find a healthy way to "fit into" your family, then you might have "kicked" your parent's values. Because you saw your parents invest heavily in their values, you knew, even if only unconsciously, that they would be hurt if you rejected what they offered. And so, to offend them, you did.

In this book's appendix, you'll find more on values. That information should help you decide which ones are really yours.

ॐॐॐ

Recall.

By now you see that there are many advantages to understanding why you're doing what you're doing when you're doing it. Remember, YOU DECIDED YOUR OWN BELIEF SYSTEM UNCONSCIOUSLY when you were a little kid under five years old. You've been on automatic pilot since. Unless you know what your "unknown pilot" believes, you aren't in charge of your behavior. Instead, your automatic pilot is giving the orders.

ॐॐॐ

Wow!

But, look, now you're reading this book and "figuring you out." And, that's great.

ॐॐॐ

More Techniques For Knowing You.

♦♦♦   General Recall About You. To get more "in touch" with your personality beliefs, try to remember anything you can about yourself from say, two years old to about eight or nine.

How did you feel most of the time: anxious or calm? Were your thoughts about yourself critical and depressing or accepting and encouraging? How did life

57

seem to you: interesting and exciting or dreadful and boring?

Do you remember comparing yourself to your brothers, sisters, cousins, or to the other kids at school? What feelings and thoughts about you or them came from that?

Can you recall your grade school teacher's attitudes toward you? Do you know what your parents felt and thought about you?

Did you feel a part of the family, really "in it," or did you stand off and watch the family from the sidelines? If you watched rather than "got in" it, how distant were you? And, why do you suppose you observed rather than participated?

It's likely that the answers to these questions describe your feelings, thoughts and behaviors today in your "now" family. Chances are likely that not much has changed in the way you perceive yourself or others. But, you can sort that out as you think about all of this.

By the way, these general memories are different from the selective memories I mention below. These recall more of the processes of your life and how those went every day. The ones I mention below are pinpoint selective.

◆◆◆   Photo Snap-Shot Memories. Now, see if you can recall some specific early memories. Remember, those before seven or eight years old are best. The ones that you choose to study should be "photo snap-shot" memories. You don't want to use ritual events, like Christmas or Thanksgiving: "Every Christmas our family did, or on Thanksgiving we always did, and so on." No, no. The ones you want are the one-moment-in-time, one-of-a-kind memories.

Look for the central theme in each recollection. Think about your memories in the same way that we

58

looked at Shannon's and Erika's and mine in the last chapter. In those we looked for patterns, repeated processes, and repeated behaviors.

Once you find that theme or those patterns, ask yourself why you behaved as you did. Ask yourself what was the purpose of your behavior: to warn, to remind, to fortify, or to teach? Or, did it have some other purpose? Here's where your belief will surface: remember that behavior comes from those deep, internal convictions.

Finally, ask yourself what your feelings were. Often, in memories, feelings are the most vital piece.

◆◆◆ Family Members. Talk with family members, even those in your extended family, such as cousins, aunts, uncles, grandparents and so on. Try to talk with a person that you or one of your parents had a close relationship with when you were a child.

Just remember that each person experiences life some differently than the next person. This happens, as you know, because each person has his own unique collection of beliefs.

◆◆◆ Old Photos or Old Movies. Look at photos of yourself and your family members. Try to recall your feelings about the situation, and the people who are in the picture. Frequently used behaviors may emerge for you. You are looking for patterns that you used back then; they are probably still with you today.

I'm sure by now you see that anything you can learn about you, or your original family will be valuable. Gradually, you will make connections between then and now. And, I hope you find learning about you to be really interesting.

ले ले ले

6. What You Give Up to Maintain Your Style.

I find this concept to be true: if you get something in life, you pay a price for it. Life rarely hands us something for nothing. On the other hand, if you give up something, often you receive a reward. Usually, there is some good in sacrifice.

This idea is important here. For every unhealthy belief you hold, you pay a price. Have you thought yet about what you sacrifice to keep your unhealthy behaviors? Let's look at some possible "prices." Then, study yourself with these ideas in mind. You may decide that the cost is too high.

The Comfort Type.

If you are the <u>exaggerated</u> Comfort type, you unconsciously insist that life be easy. So, you spend your personal resources: your time, money, and energy, to keep yourself comfortable. Maybe you haven't thought about this, but your resources are finite; they're limited. If you spend them for comfort, you can't use them to develop you. So, you've given up growth.

Or, if you look at it from the other side, and insist that you have to avoid responsibility, you prevent you from cultivating your personal gifts and talents. To achieve anything you must be willing to endure stress and pressure.

If you are the exaggerated Comfort type, you may also have sacrificed other's respect for you. They know that you are capable of much more than you are giving or doing. People think you're lazy; they don't respect you. They don't know that you have a belief system that is undermining you.

Another possible price: maybe you don't respect yourself, either. Respecting yourself means feeling good about you. Can you feel good about you when you know you are wasting yourself away? Ask yourself: does self-respect matter to me?

To be in a successful intimate relationship, you must take responsibility for your input into it, and answer the reasonable expectations of your partner. The exaggerated Comfort style thinks that any expectation is unreasonable. Of course, this is not true; a partnership of any kind takes effort. But, your

60

exaggerated Comfort style hates the whole idea of responsibility. And so, you shortchange both yourself and others because you avoid commitment.

Yet another price? Yes, very likely you are depressed. In fact, maybe you've been depressed off and on since you were in your early teens. That's when you saw yourself falling behind in your world. Some inner part of you knew that you were cheating yourself. The inner you was disappointed, sad, and angry. But, at that time, you didn't fully understand what the grownup, adult results of Comfort would look like. You just knew you weren't willing to pay the price to change your path.

Think about this. You realize large payoffs when you develop yourself. Because those bonuses are the heart of self-esteem, they're critically important. Think about the wonderful feelings you experience when you get an idea, set a goal, follow through, and complete it. Then, you know you're growing. And, you feel exhilarated about it. We need these experiences and successes to generate courage for living.

But, I understand that expanding you may seem like too much work. Yes, responsibility is something a Comfort person wants to avoid.   Even worse, now as an adult, you might think that doing life differently is impossible. I assure you, your growth is within your reach any time you want it.   Think about it now: don't you value you enough to try challenging you? I hope so.

The rest of your life is coming up.

The Pleasing Type.

If you are the <u>exaggerated</u> Pleasing type, you insist unconsciously, that you can never disappoint others; you're too afraid to jeopardize your relationships. You deeply believe that you are responsible for other's needs and wants. So, you spend your time, energy and money on them; you rarely save any of these for you.

Think about it; that means that you don't have the energy to listen to you, or to get to know or develop you. To

61

answer your own needs and develop yourself, you need those resources you've given away.   But, now they aren't available for you.   You end up with the same result as the Comfort person, lack of development, but for different reasons.

Now, about respect. Maybe you don't realize it, but you disrespect yourself when you invest so much love and care in others, and so little in yourself.   When you are so afraid of losing your relationships that you almost deplete yourself, or when your thoughts and feelings are completely about those you love, and not about your own journey, you aren't properly taking care of yourself.   You don't see yourself as equal, as deserving the same attention and investment as you give to others.   The same is true when you believe that you must provide everything your loved ones need.   You don't give yourself equal weight in your relationship. You lack self-respect.

When others see you disregard yourself for their benefit, they conclude they don't need to respect you either. Then, they usually don't. Of course, they love you. But, respecting you is another matter.   Like the Comfort person, you've probably sacrificed other's respect for you, but again, for a different reason.   People have a hard time respecting what they see as "wimpy" or "easy" or if they see you as a "pushover." They think you're weak. You create no respect there.

Ask yourself right now: what kind of relationships do I have if they are without equality and mutual respect?   There's only one answer: poor.   Are you willing to establish more balance in your life now?

Think about it; the rest of your life is coming up.

The Control Type.

If you are the <u>exaggerated</u> Control type, you believe that you can't trust people. So, you bring to every person you meet feelings of suspiciousness. You deal with people competitively, because you decided long ago that life is a contest, and you're going to win.

Your style insists that you can't stand embarrassment, surprise, humiliation or change. You deal with your fear of these feelings by controlling yourself, situations, or others to get what you want. Of course, you approach all relationships cautiously. Your only safe place is on top of others because then: YOU'RE IN CONTROL.

Because of your distrust, you rob yourself of all the good feelings that you might have if you did trust. Because you won't open to others, you taint any relationship you are in. Do you realize that when you don't share yourself, you cannot experience intimacy? Are you sure you want to pay this price?

Even though you have a partner, and maybe, even children, you're probably lonely. No, you are not actually alone, but since you never really let those you love inside you, you do not feel connected; you feel remote, distant, apart.

As for those who love you, no matter how they approach you, they can't get close. Even if they love you very much, they still must deal with your defenses: ordering them around, directing them, putting up emotional barriers that keep them out. With your need for control, people find it hard to stick around.

If you want true intimacy, you'll have to re-evaluate your beliefs, and your need for control. Ask yourself: can you let down your defenses? If you want closeness, you'll have to.

This is a good time to think about it. The rest of your life is coming up.

The Superiority Type.

If you are the <u>exaggerated</u> Superiority type, you insist unconsciously, that you "know" whatever. Because you believe that you already "know," you probably don't welcome your partner's input. If you actually try to have any intimacy in your life, you may very well come to it more as a teacher because YOU KNOW more than your partner or children.

Your style, when it's exaggerated, insists that you be "meaningful" in life. Of course, this idea takes different forms

63

with different Superiority people. But, accomplishment at a high, even lofty, level is a common theme.

Like the Control style, you don't approach people equally, not because you don't trust them, but because you're BUSY. You're on a mission to accomplish, and you can't spare any minutes for anything else. Your goals overwhelm you and your relationships. This is a price you pay when you invest so much in achievement.

Here's another price. You are nearly sick physically and emotionally from the stress of your inner demands.   All those goals! You're worn out. I see people all of the time who are exhausted, but they take for granted that exhaustion is a normal state of being. The reality? It's not.

Unfortunately, you'll probably be tired alone. In your busyness, you may have sacrificed your intimate partner. To survive, relationships need consistent focused nourishment from both participants, not just one. The person you love needs you to make the relationship a personal goal equal to all of your other ones. Do you want to do it? Yes? But, will you make the time to focus?

Every new day presents an opportunity for more balance, and so, more wholeness. When you "do" health and balance, you get the reward: intimacy.

Are you ready to re-evaluate what is most important to you? Do you want to make space in your life for those you love?

Now is the time to decide; the rest of your life is coming up.

ॐॐॐ

You can see that when your personality type is exaggerated, not balanced, you pay heavy prices.

ॐॐॐ

7. How Do Others View You?

Everyone in your family knows you better than your social friends.   Because of that, their perceptions of you may be

64

different from those who know you only casually.   Let's look at both.

The Comfort Type.

Social friends view you as charming and fun.   They see you as friendly, which you are.   They love your sense of humor. After all, when you're out for the evening, the point is to socialize and have a good time.   That you do very well.

But, those who live or work with you see you a little differently.   Early in your relationship, your light-hearted approach charms them.   But, over time, those closest to you become irritated, annoyed, and eventually, resentful and angry. The reason?   At work you don't always carry your share.   You don't like the stress and pressure.   Instead of contributing at your job, you may avoid tasks.   At home, you're likely to watch television, sleep, read or otherwise entertain yourself.   The responsibilities fall to others around you.

Over time, work partners and family members may see you as uninteresting, even boring.   If your partner wants more depth in your relationship, he may be disappointed in you IN THE LONG RUN.   He might conclude that you're comfortable relating more on the surface; you're unlikely to embrace your depth.   Your partner might grow lonely.

If you don't like these perceptions, but believe they're correct, you'll want to do something about this.   So, challenge yourself now.   Embrace personal development.   Once you experience it, you'll perceive yourself differently.   You'll enjoy the sweet reward of solid self-respect.

An extra dividend for you might be more respect from others.   Another result: a deeper, more rewarding intimate relationship.   But, the most important payoff of all is that you will feel your confidence grow.   Get going!

The Pleasing Type.

People experience you as warm, open and caring.   You give them attention, valuable help and thoughtful consideration. They perceive you as sweet and generous.   And, that is true; you are.

65

But, as people get to know you better, they see that you are also emotionally needy. They see that you'll give, give, give, without expecting anything back. They see your out-of-balance behavior when you deprive yourself and give too much to them, whether the gifts are those of time, energy or money. That's pretty uncomfortable for someone who just wants a normal give-and-take with you.

They see you at both ends of the feeling continuum. At one end, they experience you as wimpy and weak, unable to handle any amount of separateness from them. On the other end, you are strong, even controlling, as you become multi-talented to make them happy so that you don't have to feel separate.

Because Pleasers focus so much energy on maintaining a constant intimate connection with those they love, those who do not have the same goal of a constant intimate connection, may feel controlled. If you require non-stop communication, others will perceive you as "high maintenance" and might back off. Even for your partner, filling your relationship needs may be a tall order.

What was a wonderful thing initially (your partner probably felt complimented when you focused so much attention on him) may eventually become a noose around his neck (way too much of a good thing). As time goes on, he may feel impatient with so much pleasing behavior and may be thinking, "Get a life, instead of revolving around me." If your dependency persists, your partner may feel overwhelmed. After all, you're a lot of emotional responsibility.

If you want to perceive yourself differently, focus on you now. What do you want for you? Whatever it is, doing it will make you feel strong, confident and independent. Go on; go after it.

The Control Type.

When people meet you socially, they feel your strength. No uncertainty in you. You seem "in charge" and solid. They admire you very much. They feel reassured, as though they can rely on your sturdiness.

66

But, over time, those who live or work with you realize how they struggle with their feelings about you. Why? They experience you as challenging and competitive. As time goes on, partners and co-workers alike, feel stupid.

You don't value other's opinions. You have your own opinions, which you know, certainly, are the correct ones. When others around you make a decision, you probably do not honor it. You've made your decision and yours will stand. Initially, you answer requests, even harmless ones, with "No;" it's automatic.

The worst thing though, is that your partner and others feel no intimate connection with you. This is sad. Your partner concludes that he's not valued and, even worse maybe, not necessary. He reasons that if you always have everything "under control," you probably don't need a partner. Why is he in this relationship?

If you want to behave differently, listen to yourself closely for every single negative thought as it comes up. Those must be caught, understood and either tamed or discarded so that you can open to life and to others. Start this now and you will be rewarded eventually with relationship. What a payoff! But, this is true only if you value intimate connection. Do you?

The Superiority Type.

Socially, when one first meets a Superiority person, the initial reaction is one of admiration: "He's so smart" or "She accomplishes so much." These perceptions are correct. You are smart and you do get a lot done.

After awhile, though, those living or working with you feel overwhelmed with all that intensity and over-competence. They may even feel inadequate. Or, sometimes, others feel weighted down or hemmed in by your goals and your expertise. No matter what the subject, you always know the right way, the shortest way, the fastest way, the prettiest way, the least costly way or worse, all of it. You have all the bases covered because YOU KNOW. It can be really irritating to those around you. They may perceive you as "too much."

67

People who live or work with your style have trouble feeling equal, since they don't have all that intensity, or information, or goals. They may even feel inferior. Could you, a Superiority person, be sending your partner the silent message that he doesn't need to know (whatever it is) because you already have the answer? You may be saying that you don't need a real partner; maybe, you just need a decoration or a companion. After all, you've got all the other bases covered. So, he thinks, "Do I really want this kind of relationship?"

And, your partner may feel guilty. Even though he doesn't really care that he doesn't know "the right way, the most efficient way," and so on, he sometimes thinks that he should care. Well, sorry, he just doesn't. But, much of the time, especially when he's with you, he feels guilty about that.

If you want to perceive yourself differently, stop focusing on gathering all that information. Start focusing on the process between you and that other person, no matter who it is. Start seeing others as interesting. Become as curious about them as you are about your well-loved information and your goals. Make the connection between you and those you care about as much a priority as your other goals are. Cultivated carefully, your relationships can become positively absorbing.

෧෧෧

Extra Thoughts.

Your ability to set goals and your reaction to stress come next. These two pieces are pretty strong indicators of emotional health. Where are you on these scales? Wherever you are, if you're satisfied, great. If you're not satisfied, you can get where you want to be. Come on.

෧෧෧

8. *Each Type's Approach to Goal-Setting.*

The Comfort Type.

Comfort people don't like goals; they seldom think about them. All goals, whether they are short-term (the daily to-do list), medium-term (where you're going and what you're doing during the next week or month) or long-term (aiming for a college degree or for experience on a job, saving for a car, and so on), cause stress. Since Comfort people respond poorly to stress, pressure or expectations, they respond poorly to setting goals. They usually don't do it.

The Superiority Type.

At the other end of the continuum, Superiority people live their lives around their goals. Even though pressure, stress and expectations rise from objectives, so too, do suspense, anticipation, accomplishment and affirmation. To the Superiority style, pursuits are exhilarating. At an early age, Superiority people get hooked on these positive feelings, and thus, on achieving their dreams. Neither stress nor pressure outweigh the excitement.

The Pleasing Type.

Pleasing people will put all of their energy toward reaching goals; handling stress is no problem at all. But, as you know, the goals are usually someone else's, not their own.

The Control Type.

Control people fall somewhere between the extreme Comfort and extreme Superiority and Pleasing types in their response to stress. Control people do put high energy toward goals. But, because they only feel secure when they're in charge, Control people spend most of their energy controlling what is going on. Only part of their energy goes toward goals. Because there isn't much spent on moving forward, their goals get watered down. The process toward pursuits slows.

On a continuum, these style positions look like this:

0	5	10
No Goals		Heavy Goals
Extreme Comfort	Control	Extreme Pleasing/Superiority

69

❧❧❧

9. *Each Type's Reaction To Stress.*

The Comfort Type.

You already know that the Comfort person hates stress and reacts badly to it. That's because the Comfort person is easily overwhelmed. This type dreads: (1) too many tasks at the same time, (2) tasks that have to meet high standards, and/or, (3) tasks that have time pressures. Any of these are a definite problem for this type.

The Superiority Type.

At the other end of the continuum, the Superiority type responds extremely well to stress. This person learns early that he has two choices: either don't have so many goals or learn to handle pressure, time and energy well. Since goals are crucially important to the Superiority person, he learns to handle large amounts of stress early in life. However, sometimes this ability to handle pressure backfires. The Superiority type can get sick before he realizes that he has invited too much pressure into his life. Because he has learned to handle it so well, he can't feel when the pressure reaches dangerous physical levels.

The Pleasing Type.

The Pleasing type responds as well to stress as the Superiority style, often, even better. It's crucially important to Pleasers that they take care of others; they don't dare drop that ball. So, they become super-efficient. Pleasers, like Superiority people, learn time and energy management skills early and well. Then, they usually stretch all of their resources pretty thin.

Remember, even though it's a positive when people can handle stress, "good" beliefs and behaviors can turn negative when you exaggerate them.

70

The Control Type.

Controlling people generally handle stress well, as long as they can exert control over their setting and the people in it.

But, when asked whether they actually like stress or not, Controllers respond negatively. They'll put up with it, but they don't like it. That's because often, in situations that cause pressure, they're not in full control; someone else might be. And you know that not being in control is the very thing the Control person wants to avoid.

0	5	10
No Stress		Heavy Stress
Extreme Comfort	Control	Extreme Superiority/Pleasing

ৡৡৡ

By now, you should have a better idea of the unique qualities present in each style, as well as where the differences are. You are getting to know yourself better by learning which qualities are yours. That's what we want. Great!

ৡৡৡ

Reassure Yourself.

You see now that as you get better at observing yourself, you will realize when your behaviors become exaggerated. When that's the case, you should examine the beliefs that lie under your out-of-balance actions.

Further, because you want your behavior to be healthy, you'll want to change beliefs that produce exaggerated behavior. Is this possible? Yes, it is. You adopted your beliefs a long time ago without knowing that you were doing it. You can now CONSCIOUSLY drop those you don't like and develop better ones. The first step in changing is deciding that you want to. The first step in making a better life is deciding that you want it.

This idea of choosing new behavior may be a fresh one for you. And, frankly, it might seem impossible. But, it's not. Once you understand the types you've chosen, you'll understand your reasons for behaving in the way you do. Then, you can stop <u>reacting</u> and choose to be <u>pro-active</u> instead. You can make thoughtful, conscious decisions about how you will behave. You'll be in charge, not your unconscious pilot. With this new process working, you'll create an inner solid core. With time and practice comes peace.

What are other payoffs for developing this new process? When you have healthy beliefs, daily living goes smoothly. Of course, we all experience life's normal irritations. Not enough sleep, the occasional upset stomach, a cold, or the flu create upset. We sometimes must deal with unpleasant people at work. We must handle a medical emergency at home. Or, we're temporarily out of work. But broadly, through it, your relationships, intimate and social, are even and cooperative. Your work is productive. Because there is order in your inner self, there is order in your outer life. You have the time and desire to develop other areas of yourself, perhaps an unexplored talent or interest, perhaps your spiritual side. Most important of all, you'll enjoy your life's journey.

Sandy's quest led her to this spot: "I understand more every day about what's going on inside me. I'm not so confused or anxious or angry anymore. Because I understand, I choose not to REACT. Now that I know I can, I direct myself in healthy ways. Life gets better all the time." Try it; I know you can do it, too.

≈ ≈ ≈

Big Ideas From Chapter Three.

What do you know about yourself in these nine areas?
What does your partner know about himself?

1. Can you describe your temperament?

2. *Do you know your motive, your purpose?*
3. *What feelings do you dread the most?*
4. *What are your most important core beliefs?*
5. *What was your parent's role in your formation?*
6. *What do you sacrifice to keep your personality type as it is?*
7. *How do others view you?*
8. *How good are you at setting goals?*
9. *What is your reaction to stress?*

If you can answer most of these questions, you're in good shape.

The Comfort Type

Temperament: Essential qualities in my character.	I am passive. I make few demands, mind my own business, am diplomatic, relaxed, predictable, mellow, sentimental. I can be fun, entertaining, funny.
My unknown motive: What is my purpose?	I keep myself comfortable by doing what gives me pleasure.
What must I avoid?	I must avoid stress, responsibility, expectations of others and emotional or physical pain.
Some of my Core Comfort Beliefs.	**Life must be easy.** **Life must be comfortable; it must feel good.** **I don't deal with the world's reality; it's uncomfortable.** **I can make up my own reality.** **I can do life any way I want.** **I don't have to be responsible for myself emotionally (and sometimes, not physically, socially or financially either).** **Others will do it (whatever it is) for me.** **Others shouldn't ask me for anything.** **If others ask, my first response will be "No"; I'm uncomfortable with expectations.** **I don't need to say, "I'm sorry" for whatever goes wrong, even if I'm at fault.** **I can't stand pressure, stress or expectations.** **I don't have to listen.**
What parent type would encourage the formation of the Comfort type?	My parent (s) was Control or Pleasing.
What price do I pay to maintain my personality type?	I do not develop my talents and gifts. I do not find my life direction. I underachieve.
What do other people feel when they are with me?	First, they feel charmed and distracted. Later, they feel irritated and annoyed. Still later, they feel bored.

The Pleasing Type

Temperament: Essential qualities in my character.	I'm friendly, considerate, flexible, responsible, empathetic, respectful, cooperative, non-competative. I compromise; I'm likely to volunteer. I generally do what others expect.
My unknown motive: What is my purpose?	I please others to make them happy because I love them and want to connect.
What must I avoid?	I must avoid rejection, disapproval or any break in my relationships.
Some of my Core Pleasing Beliefs.	**I need someone to love and/or I need someone to love me.** **I should feel sorry for others.** **I cannot disappoint others.** **I should take care of others.** **I need someone to love, someone to be connected with.** **I should always be available for those I care about.** **My first response to requests is "Yes." can't say "No."** **I shouldn't ask for anything because that is being selfish.** **My needs and wants come last.** **I don't count.** **I must listen extremely well so that I always know what other's need.**
What parent type would encourage the formation of the Pleasing type?	My parent (s) was Pleasing or Control
What price do I pay to maintain my personality type?	I sacrifice my time and energy for other's goals. I do not develop myself.
What do other people feel when they are with me?	**First, they feel pleased that I'm a nice person. Later, they feel exasperated at my need for constant connection. Then, if I persist in unwanted pleasing, they feel controlled.**

75

The Control Type

Temperament: Essential qualities in my character.	I have leadership potential. I'm organized, productive, persistent, assertive, law abiding. I'm competitive and directive.
My unknown motive: What is my purpose?	I must control <u>myself</u> to feel safe. I must control <u>situations</u> to feel safe. I must control <u>others</u> to feel safe.
What must I avoid?	I must avoid embarrassment, ridicule, or the unexpected surprise or change.
Some of my Core Control Beliefs.	I'm right (about whatever). It's my responsibility to tell others what to do and how to do it. Others should listen to me. I should control myself, situation and/or other people to get the result I want. I can't stand to feel humiliated. I can't stand change; it interrupts my control. I can't stand surprises; they interfere with my control. I must be in charge. I can't trust others. I'm suspicious of intimate relationships because I can't totally trust. My first response to requests will be "No". I don't have to listen; I already know.
What parent type would encourage the formation of the Control type?	**My parent (s) was Control, Pleasing or Comfort.**
What price do I pay to maintain my personality type?	I lack spontaneity. I lack closeness in my relationships. I don't develop my softer side, my creativity.
What do other people feel when they are with me?	**First, they feel tension, resistance and challenged, then, lonely and sad.**

The Superiority Type

Temperament: Essential qualities in my character.	I seek many goals. I'm knowledgeable, precise, industrious, thorough, idealistic. I seek perfection. I'm persistent, orderly, responsible and have a strong moral sense of right and wrong.
My unknown motive: What is my purpose?	I try to be very competent, very good, right and ethical. I try to be very useful and proper.
What must I avoid?	I must avoid meaninglessness in life. I must avoid feelings of worthlessness and boredom.
Some of my Core Superiority Beliefs.	**I know (whatever) because I love Information.** **I must make some meaningful contribution to life.** **I must treat life seriously.** **I must be responsible.** **I must always do the right thing.** **I must figure life out.** **I can't do anything half way; it must be done thoroughly.** **I must be precise, accurate, and maintain high standards and so must others.** **I can do it all; all my goals.** **My first response to requests can be "Yes," or "No."** **I can't wait or slow down; I'm too busy.** **I don't have time to listen.**
What parent type would encourage the formation of the Superiority type?	**My parent(s) was Superiority, Pleasing, or Comfort. They were parents who shamed.**
What price do I pay to maintain my personality type?	I feel over-burdened, over-committed and over-involved, because I am.
What do other people feel when they are with me?	First, they feel admiration. Later, they feel inadequate because they don't have the same goals. Then, some may feel guilty because they don't have the same intense high standards.

77

Anything in life worth having is worth working for.

ৡ   ৡ   ৡ

Chapter Four

Balance

Balance—What Is It?

*I*n the first section of this chapter, there are four examples given, one for each personality type. In each case, you'll see a person whose behavior is extremely out-of-balance; the actions are exaggerated. After that person's awareness rises about his imbalance, you'll see him back himself up to a point of balance in his style, then in his behavior. He saw the harm and wanted change.

In the last section of this chapter, we focus on another kind of balance: equality among all four types. Once you pull each of your two styles into a more balanced place, then you can focus on including your other two less important styles into your everyday living.

For instance: now, you might be so heavy in Pleasing and Superiority that positive Control and Comfort are entirely left out of your daily behavior. Let's say your Superiority directs you to work toward your goals all the time. So, you don't plan fun or entertainment. Then, you have no release from responsibility and work. And, let's say that because you are an extreme Pleaser, you don't know how to say "no" to others. In addition to working on your own goals, you're working on other's goals, too. You aren't limiting the time and energy you spend. You have little control over yourself and, sooner or later, you'll suffer because of it.

Or, you can be very heavy in Comfort and Control to get the Comfort (manipulation). You don't set goals (Superiority) or have a good life structure (Control over your environment), to support you. If you have little to no Pleasing, you're distant in your relationships. You'd be smart to include these in your life because doing so would make your life better.

You see, it doesn't matter which styles you own, or even how positive your top two are, if your behavior doesn't include all four, it isn't as healthy as it should or could be.

ॐ ॐ ॐ

Each Type Within Itself Healthy.

Let's look at each personality type again. But, in this chapter, let's look at them as though they each run on a scale from unhealthy to healthy, from negative to positive. You see, you can use your types in either way, positive or negative.

We'll look at what negative behavior looks like for each type. If you can recognize unhealthy movement, you can stop it. That's what you want.

ॐ ॐ ॐ

The Comfort Type.

Stephanie's Story.

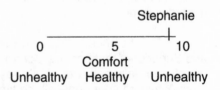

Stephanie and Jim had been dating for twelve years (yes, 12), and Stephanie wanted to get married. They'd talked about marriage for the last two years, but Jim always hesitated about setting the date. She wanted to marry or move on.

Stephanie claimed she didn't know why Jim was delaying. But, he insisted that he had told her why he wouldn't commit. He thought she just wouldn't accept it. She couldn't allow herself to hear the reasons; they threatened her too much. Acknowledging those meant she would have to change some of her Comfort behavior. But, Stephanie asked herself, "Why would she want to do that?" To her, this sounded like Jim's problem.

It wasn't until Jim said that he was afraid to marry her that she began to listen. His mention of "fear" startled her. Stephanie asked herself, "Why would Jim be afraid of me?" His answer: He didn't think he could live with Stephanie acting so irresponsibly day after day. Already he felt disgusted and frustrated with her; already he had lost some respect for her. He worried that those ugly feelings would heighten and diminish his love for her. "Okay," Stephanie finally asked him, "What are you talking about?"

This. When Stephanie feels depressed or anxious, she rushes to comfort herself. Mostly, she goes shopping and spends. Or, she sleeps, overeats, runs to the movies or watches television. The one thing she doesn't do is face the real problem. Instead, she reacts to her anxiety.

What creates this anxiety? Her original beliefs about how life should be create the anxiety. They are so different from life's realities. Stephanie doesn't like normal daily demands. She doesn't like balancing her checkbook, ironing her clothes, cooking meals, or anything else that isn't easy or fun. Remember, her core beliefs are: "I can make my own reality," "Life must be easy," " Someone else will do it," "What matters in life is feeling good NOW." With these beliefs, she insulates herself against adult responsibilities, even though she's 51 years old.

To make it worse, all of her comfort habits dilute her anxiety and create good feelings "now." For this reason, she can't see anything wrong with them. She can even argue that the way she copes distracts her. It helps her feel better; so, she concludes it's a good thing to do.

Here's the reality. When you have a checking account, you need to balance it. When you wear clothes, you must take care of them. At mealtime, if you expect to eat, you must cook. If someone else is going to do these jobs for you, you must arrange that, and earn the money to pay them. You cannot just let responsibilities go undone.

So, we see Stephanie is missing two things: (1) accountability beliefs and the attitudes and actions that come from those, and (2) the practical skills she needs to carry out life's obligations: thinking, assessing problems, choosing solutions, initiating, following through, reaching closure, and so on.

Sadly, when a child builds Comfort beliefs, those ideas almost guarantee that later in elementary school years, the child will miss out on building the life skills he needs as an adult. We know that the beliefs grow during the birth to four or five year-old time, and we also know that the child develops specific life skills from five on through to adulthood. But, in the Comfort style, the child's beliefs actually direct the child, then later, the adult, away from work and accountability. As you know, learning any skill is work. So, it doesn't make sense to the Comfort child to try to gain skills that at an unconscious level he never expects to need. He expects life's demands to be taken care of by others. What would he need skills for? Does this thinking seem complicated? Yes, though thinking it through, you see the Comfort child's logic. It makes sense.

On the other hand, when a child builds beliefs like: "I can handle this (whatever it is)," "I'll do it myself," "Learning is fun," "I want to do it, too," as they grow up, they learn life skills, mostly because they set goals. Unconsciously, the child understands that if he's going to have goals and move forward he needs to know how to reach them. Thus, he learns how to "do."

Stephanie never got to this point. So, when situations arise that make her feel bad, she reaches for old solutions. She buys more stuff, or she hibernates. Here we have the Comfort style at its worst.

Also, when Stephanie operates on the negative side of her style, she always damages not only herself, but also Jim. When you're part of a couple, the way you use your time, energy, and money affects your partner as it affects you. Why? You and your partner share responsibilities and resources.

Jim's style is the opposite of Stephanie's. He knows that the only effective way to handle life is to face it, and walk through it. He doesn't avoid it. Is this hard for him to do? Sometimes. But, as a child he grew beliefs that urge him to face the real world's demands even though that may be difficult. He knows that when you pay that price, you get solid rewards: improved skills, confidence in yourself, and a stronger willingness to handle the next problem. This process is the core of self-esteem.

For Jim, it's so painful to watch Stephanie not deal with the roots of her inner anxiety and confusion. Watching her ignore life's requests scares him; he sees the results.

What's more, Stephanie's "coping" behaviors have sent her credit card balances sky high. Her "spending habit" means that if she and Jim marry, his long-term goals: funding his kids' college education or investing in a larger home or saving for retirement, won't be met. His fear for their future makes sense.

Jim's been angry with Stephanie for a long time. And even though he loves her, he doesn't want to live with her self-indulgent behavior. He wants the person he marries to be responsible and cooperative.

Later, as our therapy continued, Stephanie finally got the idea. She began to get serious about understanding herself: in particular, why she had always tried so hard to avoid any emotional unpleasantness or practical responsibility. Then, she finally embraced the personal goal of change.

At first, she did this for Jim. Then, once she realized how good it felt to spend her energy facing a problem down and getting on top of it, she jumped into it for her own tremendous personal payoff. These days, she doesn't run away anymore.

∂∽∂∽∂∽

83

The Pleasing Type.

Todd's Story.

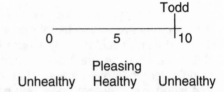

Todd

0   5   10

Pleasing
Unhealthy   Healthy   Unhealthy

I met Todd just after his divorce from his second wife, Adrienne. Still grieving over the loss of his marriage, he wanted to understand why two marriages had ended badly. He had invested heavily in both. Two failures just didn't make sense to him.

Todd and Sara, his first wife, married while they were still in college. Sara's type is Comfort, like Todd's mother. (I find this to be true, generally: We are more like one parent and unconsciously choose a version of our other parent for a life partner). With Sara, Todd played out the Pleasing beliefs he had formed by watching his dad with his mom: "I can't disappoint those I love," "I'm responsible for those I love," and so on.

Todd's other personality type is Superiority, again formed because he imitated his father. Some of his beliefs here are: "I have many goals," "I'm interested in lots of things," "I will work hard at whatever I do."

Early in the marriage, he developed a successful import/export business that made very good money. Even though it meant working hard, Todd took care of Sara and their three young children both financially and emotionally. They all lived well.

Todd's dad always protected his Mom, him and his younger sister and brother. Todd thought relationship should be done in this way because in his original home that was how it went.

Ten years and three children later, Sara wanted out of the marriage. Todd, who hadn't seen this coming, was blindsided. And, heartbroken. Following a bitter divorce and custody battle, the marriage ended. Todd had no idea why.

◆ Balance ◆

Todd picked up the pieces of his life and got on with it. Soon after, he met and married Adrienne. Even though they dated for two years, he didn't see that she was very like Sara. She needed and expected to be taken care of, as Sara had. He just knew he loved her and she felt "right" to him.

As for Adrienne, in Todd she saw a strong, capable, intense, but sensitive man. He was open and flexible. And miraculously, he believed in giving instead of taking. In her, he saw a charming, pretty, friendly person who loved him, and who appreciated all he did for her. All looked and felt good to both of them.

The marriage ended l8 years later. Adrienne had grown tired of Todd. She wanted a man who didn't bore her. So, she found another partner, Gordon. Not having seen the break coming, Todd was devastated.

Why had this happened? Over the years, Adrienne's respect for Todd dwindled; he didn't act as though he respected himself. What was he doing wrong?

We soon found out. Even the pain of his second divorce hadn't diminished Todd's desire for a lasting relationship. So, he began to date again. As we watched him court various women, we saw his unhealthy, excessive Pleasing quickly. That was good; we could study it.

In ten month's time, Todd went through four dating "relationships." Fortunately for him, none of these worked out. This, in spite of the fact that he's handsome, physically fit, makes a good living, has deep positive values, and is an all-around nice guy. What was going on?

Keep in mind that Todd believed: "I need this relationship." "I can't disappoint others," and "I'm ultimately responsible for those I care about." So, when Todd met a woman, he'd shower her with frequent phone calls, invitations, flowers, notes, cards and more phone calls. Whatever she wanted or needed, he provided right now. Very quickly, Todd would overwhelm, and yes, often scare or even bore his current woman.

85

With his behavior Todd sent an unconscious but blatant invitation that had "Take advantage of me!" written all over it. He also had a belief that if the relationship in his life wasn't working, it must be his fault. Then, his belief "I must try harder" kicked in. In other words, he took on all of the responsibility.

Todd's willingness to be responsible, and his eagerness for a loving connection made him a sitting duck. The woman would misinterpret Todd's generosity for weakness. You would think that Todd's partner would admire his behavior, but no, she didn't. Todd got little in return for what he gave. Obviously, he looked and felt emotionally needy; he was.

You can see that there was no balance in Todd's Pleasing behavior. He didn't give himself the same care and respect that he gave his partner. That was because Todd didn't know anything about self-respect. He learned how to do intimate relationships by watching his dad. Neither his dad nor he knew about limiting generosity, respecting himself, or about achieving balance.

Now, Todd sees that when he gives too much too soon, he makes himself too vulnerable. When he gives too much, he makes himself unimportant in the relationship. Others judge him to be weak.

Now, he also knows that even though he has no desire to control his partner (his motive isn't to have power over her, it's simply to be with her), he realizes that on her side it may feel suffocating. Overall, he's just wiser now about how his behavior is interpreted.

These days Todd is more patient. He moderates his Pleasing behavior.

Also, he "reads" other people better now. Remember, earlier I wrote that if you learned these four personality types well, you would understand not only yourself, but also others much better. As you learn more and more about the styles, you should be able to tell what is coming at you. Instead of reacting to other's behavior, you can evaluate it, and be proactive with yours.

86

Now, Todd can look back to prior relationships and see how skewed his behavior was, and he disciplines himself against that. He reads facial expressions and body language. He thinks about a woman's motive behind her call, visit or request. Before he acts, he thinks about his own motives, and whether or not it would be wise to act on them. Overall, he's smarter about relationship. This is all positive, and, of course, it's healthy because it's more balanced. Now, his behavior takes care of both him and the other person in his life. It doesn't leave room for misinterpretation.

Todd is dating a woman that he cares about. Betty seems right for him; he's excited about where this might lead. But, he is careful to use his Pleasing style in a diluted way. He respects the boundaries between the two of them. As a result, Betty treats him with respect and equality. She sincerely values him. We know it's because he's finally respecting and valuing himself. His behavior is balanced.

Keep your eye on all of the process steps here. First, Todd looked at himself. He recognized that his behavior produced negatives. Second, in studying himself, he identified unhealthy beliefs. Third, he learned to recognize people and situations that hooked up his unconscious beliefs and negative behaviors. Fourth, he learned to "catch himself" while doing his unhealthy Pleasing. Fifth, little by little, he stopped. Finally, he built a new process to achieve his goal. It's really paying off for him.

ﭬﭬﭬ

The Control Type.

Michael's Story.

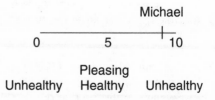

Beth came to my office anxious and depressed. I could see why. Michael, Beth's husband of twenty years, dominated their home, their social life, their finances, her and their two daughters, Amy and Laura. Because of Michael's constant oppression, Beth was falling apart, both emotionally and physically. She was taking antidepressants and muscle relaxants just to cope. Because of some miserable years, Beth's love for Michael had dwindled until there was hardly any left. She felt no sexual desire for him and no emotional energy for the relationship. This was a marriage in crisis.

Let's take a look at Michael's early development.

As a little guy and until Michael turned 25 years old, his mom and dad owned a neighborhood bar-poolroom. The bar generated good money, a lot of it in cash.

From a young age, Michael hung around the bar; his parents often took him to work with them. Later, Michael began working there. He continued until he was out of high school. Consequently, he always had cash. And, he heard daily from his mom how important it was to work hard at making money. His mother told him over and over: "Take care of your money," and "Stay out of debt; pay cash for everything." In this family, the spotlight on money was strong.

In Michael's original family, his mother controlled the money. She called the shots; she decided almost everything about all family issues. His dad played the passive partner; he followed his wife's lead. Michael "watched and imitated" his mother's personality style. In his marriage, he was the active partner, Beth, the passive one. Of course, for Michael, his behavior made perfect sense. What was Beth's problem?

Michael's been obsessed with money his entire adult life. That obsession has loomed as a constant problem in his marriage. Over time, his anxiety has actually grown instead of diminished.

He insists that: (1) Beth turn over her entire paycheck to him every payday, (2) each bill be paid as soon as it comes in (no waiting until the due date), (3) the family cannot have any debt no matter how small; it makes him feel threatened and unsafe, (4) none of them can spend money on clothes, hobbies, vacations; it decreases his savings. His beliefs that: "I'll never have enough money," "I can't owe anybody anything," "I must keep total control of all of my resources," and so on, internally pushed him around. And then, through Michael's actions, they pushed Beth and their daughters around too. Because his beliefs produced exaggerated feelings and behavior, everybody in this household was miserable.

What's the financial reality for Michael and Beth? They both work at well-paying jobs. Beth is a teacher and Michael works as a maintenance man for the local city parks. His job security is high; everyday he increases his seniority. And, the city provides great insurance and retirement benefits. Their $250,000 house is completely paid for, even though they are both only in their early forties. And, they each have good retirement investments, as well as savings accounts.

Michael behaves as though none of these assets exist. His early belief system dominates, making his inner "reality" false. But, because his beliefs are so strong, no amount of assurance that he has enough money makes any difference to Michael. No amount of money will ever make him feel safe, because his behavior is not about money. Its root is an internal feeling of insecurity. He believes that having money will eliminate this feeling. It won't. At its foundation, his fear is irrational.

Michael tries controlling in other ways, too. He's also driven to control the environment he's in.

For example, he insists his house look perfect all the time. Nothing can ever be out of place or the slightest bit dusty. The family can't entertain; something might get broken or scratched.

Beth spoke up: "Our possessions are made to be used," and "Our belongings will eventually wear out and we should expect to replace them." Michael strongly resisted these ideas. Frowning, he would reply, "Replacing things takes money. I'm not spending my money like that. You know, I wouldn't have to, if you would do what I tell you: be careful."

89

Again, Beth's reality statement, "Michael, the girls and I want to entertain, if only occasionally. And, we want to be able to relax and not worry so much about our stuff," was met with, "I don't care if you're relaxed or not. You're not going to ruin our furniture." His unhealthy beliefs strangled other possibilities as Beth's words were spoken. When anyone challenged Michael's rigid beliefs, his anxiety rose to choke him.

And, unfortunately, Michael's control showed up in still other places, too. As you will see, it pervaded every place he entered.

Over the years Michael has refused to go out socializing because they might spend too much money. Beth loves to dance and see new movies. But, Michael kept their evenings out to a bare minimum by refusing to go. Early in the marriage, Beth wouldn't go without him. But, in the last five years, she has gone out with friends more and more, even if he refuses.

At times, if Michael knew that Beth was going out without him, he'd relent and go along. But, even then, he controlled the situation. Sometime during the evening he'd insult her or someone else. For Beth, it didn't seem worth it to plan an evening out, just to be embarrassed. Or, Michael would deliberately get drunk. What Beth hoped would be a fun evening out would turn into a bad dream; she'd have to drive him home and struggle him into bed.

At other times, when she does go on without him, he makes her pay for it by creating an awful scene when she comes home. He calls her names and throws lamps and other things around; it frightens her. When he started following her from room to room pushing and shoving her, she decided enough was enough.

Has his fear, anxiety and control cost him anything besides, possibly, his wife and daughters. Yes. Michael has suffered from spastic colitis off and on for about ten years. Just before he came to see me, he started taking his medication again. His colitis had come back strong. His migraines began again full force, too, and the medicine prescribed for those wasn't working. His body scared him. Rightfully so. It was sending his belief system a message loud and clear. "I can't handle any more stress from your anxiety; get a grip on yourself."

You can probably see by now, that the one kind of control Michael lacked was Control Over Self. That, he desperately needed. Inside, he was as miserable as Beth and the girls were, but for different reasons.

When I began to work with Michael, he had some pretty rigid defenses, as you can imagine. He admitted to feeling an enormous amount of anxiety; it controlled him and at the same time, it terrified him. He understood that his anxiety pushed him around internally 24 hours a day. Yes, he understood that it was the reason he pushed Beth and the girls around. Then, why did he do it? Simple; it lessened his anxiousness when he had everything and everybody under control.

But then, he loved Beth and didn't want her to leave him. So, he agreed to work on himself.

Over time, Michael was moderately successful at controlling the anxiety. He and I worked to release the original beliefs that drove his irrational, scary behavior. Little by little, Michael's controlling actions diminished. As he dropped his old beliefs, we formed new, more balanced ones. Michael also calmed his body and his inner atmosphere by learning more about physical fitness, practicing deep-breathing exercises, and taking medication for a year while he developed some new behaviors.

Over time, Beth stopped threatening to leave him. Even though he would never give up all of his controlling behavior, she decided she could handle what was left of it. He's better now at treating her and the girls with more respect. He's better at partnering. She decided that she would continue the marriage, and try to make it work again.

Michael will always be concerned about money. Because of that, he'll want to control people and situations. But, he's counting on his growing self-discipline to help him with his strong controlling impulses. He still doesn't like surprises; he still hates change. But, he knows now that he owns strong irrational beliefs; he knows that they've hurt him and his family. So, he continues looking inward to understand his belief structure, and to drop off old, corrupt beliefs when he finds them. He is striving for balance.

ॐॐॐ

The Superiority Type.

Eric's Story.

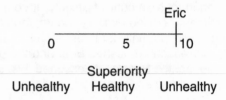

A shocked Eric arrived at my office the day after he'd had a visit to the emergency room of a nearby hospital. The doctors there assured him that no, he had not had a heart attack; he'd had an anxiety attack. All he knew was that whatever it was, it had felt awful. Now, he was terrified it would happen again. Before it did, he wanted to know exactly what was going on, and what to do about it.

So, we started on Eric's journey of self-discovery. Eric, a first-born child, is independent, intense. He's driven by excess energy, which he funnels into goals of all kinds everywhere in his life. Eric's always in movement, moving ahead, moving up, moving into new projects, moving to avoid boredom, moving to accomplish something, always moving.

Eric's style is like his dad's. As a little boy, Eric watched his dad work two jobs and also be involved with projects on the weekends. Eric grew beliefs like, "Life is exciting and interesting," "I want to accomplish," "I can do it all," and "I have to hurry to get everything done."

Eric started his busyness early. At seven years old he made a model sailboat from scratch, entered it in a contest and won first prize. By eleven, he was handy enough with tools to finish his parent's basement family room.

At age eighteen he enrolled in college to become an architect. But, he quit in his junior year; he was anxious to get on with his life. So, seventeen years ago at the age of twenty, Eric started his painting and wallpapering business. It has grown; he now employs fourteen people.

The urgent question now is: how has he gotten to this point in his life? He's jeopardizing his health.

In childhood Eric's parents encouraged him to pursue the goals he chose. They never gave him the message that he should slow down. To the contrary, they saw his interests as good; after all, his father lived a very productive work life.

Now, years later, even though Jan, his wife, knew how much "moving forward" meant to him, she discouraged him from taking on so much work. She saw how he drove himself. Even so, she didn't want to nag him about working too hard. But then, they had the surprise hospital visit. Now, she felt really scared.

So, Eric and I started looking at his daily schedule to see where he spent his time. By studying his movements, we could be pretty clear about what his beliefs were.

His day started at 5:00 a.m. when the alarm went off. It ended around 11:30 p.m. when he turned off his reading light. He spent the hours between 5:00 a.m. and 7:00 a.m. getting ready for work, eating breakfast, and making phone calls to his various job foremen. From 7:00 a.m., when he left for work until 5:00 p.m. when he arrived back home, he drove from site to site managing his employees, or he helped on a job. Once home, he'd fix dinner for the family. He, Jan and Joel would eat, and he'd play with his two-year-old for 30 minutes or so. Then, he'd go downstairs to work on his current project.

He scheduled his time so tightly every day that there wasn't a moment free from intense goals. Eric's beliefs had programmed him to feel heavy internal pressure to achieve. "So?" Eric thought, "I've always felt that way." It never occurred to him that he shouldn't live this; it never occurred to him that living every minute under pressure wasn't "normal."

93

I soon learned that Eric's problem wasn't just that he took on too much work, filling every minute of every day. Yes, he did. But, also, he held high standards and aimed for perfection. So, he spent time and energy redoing work that by more usual and balanced standards would have been fine. This applied both to work that he did for others in his business and work that he did for himself, too.

Soon, Jan joined us. Her view of life differed from Eric's. She worked as an outside salesperson, she sold computer parts to large companies. Clearly, she had a demanding job. But, her approach to work differed from her husband's. She worked between 30 and 35 hours a week but wasn't willing to do more than that. She spent her remaining time on their son, their home and social life and on taking care of herself. She didn't even think about perfection. She contented herself with doing a good job. Actually, she had a fairly relaxed approach to daily living. She balanced her life pretty well.

In one of her first visits with me, Jan revealed some feelings she had tried from time to time to tell Eric about. She often felt lonely. During their courtship, Eric and Jan spent almost all of their time together. But, shortly after their wedding, Eric went back to his many projects. Again, when their son, Joel, came, Eric stayed involved for a while. But soon, he drifted away, back to his work. Jan felt cheated. But, when she talked with Eric about it, he just couldn't hear her.

Now, Eric agreed to observe himself. He noticed that when he was out with Jan, he couldn't just breathe easy and have a good time. Instead, this mind continually worked generating business ideas. Gradually, he understood that because he paid attention to his constant thoughts, and not to what was going on between them, he cheated their relationship. He was always in his own mind, rather than with Jan; he was not "present." To really listen, you must be present and focused.

Examining his behavior, Eric saw that he sought perfection in his relationships, too. Rather than just enjoying his son, he'd have goals for Joel to reach when they were together. Joel's progress preoccupied Eric, and he usually played the role of "teacher" to the exclusion of "father."

94

Eric wore his teacher hat with Jan often, too. He tried to teach her better ways of doing the vacuuming, the cleaning and the cooking or whatever. In other words, he had trouble just hanging out with Jan and Joel. In fact, he couldn't relax anywhere.

So, we worked for balance. Finally, Eric accepted the truth that, like everyone else, he had only 24 hours a day, (a harsh reality to any Superiority type person). This truth would prevail no matter how hard he pushed or how anxious he became. Contrary to a common Superiority MISbelief, anxiety does not make you move faster, and it does not make you more productive. The Superiority person's enormous energy and his "wanting to accomplish," produce the harvest.

Gradually, little by little, Eric retrained himself. He slowed his racing thoughts; he learned to discipline his intense feelings. And, he moderated his behavior.

Slowly, he learned to own his goals, instead of letting them own him. He lowered his expectations of himself and Jan and Joel. Now, he takes small breaks during his work-day so that his mind rests. He practices deep-breathing exercises while he's driving, instead of planning his next project. In general, he takes better care of himself and those in his life. So, for now, he's in good shape emotionally and physically because he practices better balance.

෨෨෨

All Four Styles Balanced and Blended Together.

Let's take another look at balance, but from that second perspective. Now, we're focused on the balance you achieve when you blend the four personality types reasonably equally. If you look at the positive aspects of each style, you'll see that you need them all. If you build this balance among the four types, you'll be able to handle whatever life situations you encounter with courage and resourcefulness.

෨෨෨

The Comfort Type.

Because comfort rejuvenates the mind and body, it should have an important place in our lives. Entertainment relieves stress; it acts as a critical release valve for tension and pressure. When you work continuously, as the Pleasing and Superiority styles do, you risk ill health, emotionally, physically or both. So, whatever healthy fun activity you like that diverts you from serious to lighthearted, you should do it. Play frees your spirit and promotes laughter. You want that. Not only is relaxing good for you but sharing humor builds smart relationships. Just being silly together builds trust between you and your partner.

But, on the other hand, too much comfort in your life, either alone or with your partner can be addictive and dangerous. You've seen a good example of out-of-control Comfort with Stephanie. And, I haven't mentioned yet any of the obvious addictions like alcohol, various drugs, eating, gambling, and so on.

If you have too much Comfort in your style, seek balance. Strive for evenness in your life. Balance always aims for the middle ground. So, what does that mean? One, you must increase your ability to do responsibility in its many forms: in work duties and with intimate and social relationships. To balance the tendency toward excessive comfort, set daily goals, and work to achieve whatever means something to you. You will feel good; that's your payoff. These good feelings increase little by little, resulting eventually in self-confidence. With your increasing confidence, you encourage yourself emotionally, intellectually, socially, and in other unseen ways. In other words, this process makes a positive upward spiral.

Two, think of the others in your life at the same time you are filling your own needs. When you consider your partner's wants and needs, as you consider your own, you interrupt your tendency toward self-centeredness. Thinking of others as you do yourself does result in balance because it completes the relationship circle.

ॐॐॐ

The Pleasing Type.

Because we live in a social world, pleasing behavior is essential for "fitting in" in it. It's important that you get along with others, and cooperate to do what is needed in whatever situation you're in. If you think about your daily life, you'll see that you're already using pleasing behavior.

But, if you excessively take care of others because you're afraid you'll lose a relationship, then your behavior isn't balanced. Remember Todd? No, none of that; balance is what you're striving for.

Also, if you've been over-pleasing, you must learn to share responsibility, instead of assuming it's always yours. Don't take on a task just to "please," or to take care of others, without seriously evaluating whether the task is yours or someone else's. Take on tasks because they need to be done or because it brings you pleasure to do them, not because you want to serve someone. In other words, you do your part, then step back to let others do theirs. Eventually, after practicing, you should feel okay about refusing responsibility that belongs elsewhere. This is healthy Pleasing.

Don't forget that you're aiming for balance. You achieve that when you think of yourself as equal to others, not more capable and not more needy. You retain your equality by expecting respect, as you give respect to others. You've seen that nobody respects the person who doesn't respect himself. When you feel self-respect and know what you need and want, it balances your need to please others. Go ahead; get started practicing.

ल ल ल

The Control Type.

Think about what your life would be like without you having some control over it. Pretty chaotic. You probably feel high anxiety when your internal atmosphere or your physical surroundings are in chaos. It is hard to be responsible, never mind creative, in a turbulent environment, whether that turmoil is in your physical surroundings or in your relationships.

97

Control over Self.

Do you realize that you are irresponsible when you allow you to REACT to situations that come up in your life? It's true. Behaving without thinking eventually leads to disorder, confusion and turmoil inside you and in your relationships.

At the other end of the continuum, you could control yourself so completely that you emotionally hide from others and, yes, even hide from yourself. The middle ground? Move forward with proactive behavior after reflection. That's the balance.

Rigid Self-Control is Unhealthy	Balance Healthy	Total Spontaneity is Unhealthy

Does this reflecting before speaking or acting seem contrived or unnatural? It isn't, but it might feel that way if your actions have been impulsive REactions. Spontaneity is often a word used to defend the freedom to say or do whatever a person wishes whenever he wishes. That works if you don't care about your partner's feelings. But, if you value your relationship, then your talk and behavior must be the responsible kind. That way, you preserve your partnerships.

Control over Environment.

Positive Control Over Your Environment simply means that the "stuff in your life," your belongings, is in reasonable order. Taking control over your things decreases your anxious feelings. If you try this, you'll see what I mean.

But, if you exert this control, your behavior should respectfully consider other's feelings, thoughts, space and roles. Establishing order in your home and your workplace results in an inner calm that benefits everyone. If this idea has never occurred to you, try it now.

Control over Others.

Controlling other people is, at its core, a corrupt idea. Its essence is vertical dominance by one partner over the other; it makes open equality impossible. Overpowering control doesn't belong in respectful relationships.

Furthermore, you can't control your partner into doing what you want, even if what you want is good. He must decide on his own to act; he must make that choice himself.

But, you've got some powerful tools when you try to influence those you love to do positive things: respectful language, good leadership and coaching skills, your own positive behavior as a model, and encouragement. Also, when you refuse to direct others, and instead, set your personal boundaries around behavior you will or will not allow in your space, you set a mighty model for sturdy wholeness. When you use these approaches rather than aggression, you're promoting smart relationship.

With your partner you should maintain an understanding attitude, and you should look for that same attitude to come back to you. Together, aim for level problem solving. Partners who use their energy to work for solutions rather than winning through control, usually succeed in preserving and enhancing the relationship, as well as solving problems.

The Superiority Type.

Superiority beliefs make sure that you set goals and that you feel the desire and have the energy to follow them through. When you meet your goals through your own unique effort, you experience the satisfaction that builds personal power. You grow more confident every time you positively meet the challenges that come along, most especially those presented by daily living. As your self-trust and your confidence grow, you feel less anxious, calmer, more sure that you will meet life and relationship needs and demands successfully.

99

Yes, it is good if a person has a Superiority style with behaviors of hard work, ingenuity, and high energy, as long as that person also balances those behaviors with: (1) good self-control: not overworking and neglecting his relationships, (2) positive Control over his environment: order and calm, (3) enough Pleasing so that he can cooperate with others, and (4) creative Comfort: healthy fun and relaxation.

ॐॐॐ

Look around you and see if you know anyone you would consider really balanced. It's very likely that that person works hard at achieving goals (Superiority), is self-composed and lives an orderly life, not one in crisis or chaos, (Control), is one who cooperates well with others, but can "hold his own" (Pleasing), and has favorite pastimes that bring pleasure in non-work hours (Comfort). Now, you see that combining all four styles, well balanced and blended, is the healthiest lifestyle to develop.

ॐ   ॐ   ॐ

Big Ideas From Chapter Four.

1. *Define Balance.*
2. *Move to balance your behavior within each of your two heaviest styles.*

Comfort	Control
Ex: 0_____ 10	0_____ 10
5	*5*
Balance	*Balance*

3. *Move to balance all four styles in your life.*

Comfort	Control
Pleasing	*Superiority*

Balance among all

Enjoy your newly developed evenness and calmness.

It isn't what a man does
that gives him value. It is what he is.

ๅ   ๅ   ๅ

Part Two

About
Relationships

*Unless knowledge is converted into action, then
wisdom, it will become stagnant, like still water.*

ɚ   ɚ   ɚ

Chapter Five

Communication

Are You A Smart Communicator?

*H*ow many times have you heard or read that communication makes a good relationship? Plenty, I bet. Often clients come to a first session convinced that their relationship problem is poor communication. Can I help them fix it? Yes, if we agree on what makes communication.

So, what is it? Is communication talking? Yes. Isn't it also listening? Yes! And, much more.

In our normal, everyday talking, we pass information to each other. And, we usually understand the messages because at the surface level they are easy to get.

But, aware of it or not, you send other silent messages, along with the words you speak. And, when others talk to you, they, too, send soundless data along with their spoken words.

It is in these quiet, deeper layers that more serious and important relationship happens. Your motives for speaking, your attitudes about others, and your feelings about yourself and your partner emerge when you speak. You may not be consciously aware of these subtle layers. Neither is your partner, maybe. But, they are there.

If you want to communicate well, get to know your own process in these unknown layers. You don't want to be unconsciously sending messages that you don't know you're sending. No, you want to be a smart communicator who understands yourself well enough to own and intend the messages you send out.

So, in this chapter, we'll focus on how to say what you mean, and also preserve your significant relationship. We'll focus on learning this complicated process called communication.

ॐॐॐ

Talking.

First: Talk Plainly. *** To be a good information "sender," you must know why you are speaking. This comment may sound silly, but if you listen carefully, you'll hear yourself and others talking unnecessarily. If you aren't sure about the purpose of your message, your partner, too, will be uncertain why you are talking. If he's thinking about all those words coming at him rather than what you're actually meaning, he won't get your message. Sheer volume is intimidating.

Also, when you are "present" to yourself, you know why you are speaking. You can choose whether to talk or not. Does this sound foolish? Well, have you ever caught yourself saying things you wish you hadn't? That's probably because you aren't listening to yourself or filtering your thoughts. You aren't present to you. If you are not present, there's no way you can be responsible for the words coming out of your mouth; you haven't thought about them. So, try not to speak thoughtlessly. Ask yourself: "What is my motive here?"

Second: Be Sparse. *** Say only what you mean. How many times have you started to talk about one topic and ended up talking about that and a few more? If you're typical, it happens more than you want it to. When this occurs, you may not make your point clear. So, stay focused.

Also, listen to yourself as you speak and select out any "noise." "Noise," anything other than your core message, may confuse your listener. You don't want to muddy your issue.

Third: Be Clear. *** Use language that is direct and respectful. When you use guarded language, others feel manipulated. You want the opposite of that; you're striving to protect the connection you have with your partner. You don't want to generate bad feelings.

If the two of you don't have a close connection now, do these processes anyway. Being respectful and clear creates confidence in you, and hope in your partner. Open talk promotes trust and, thus, closeness, quicker than any other kind.

If you develop these speaking habits, you will avoid feeling annoyed or frustrated. And, you will not have to say, "I didn't mean that," or "You misunderstood me," so often.

Listening.

First: Listen for purpose. *** The other half of any exchange is the listening part. To be a good "receiver," concentrate on fully understanding what your partner is saying. This means not just hearing the subject, the content he's talking about, but also tuning into what process he uses. To get his message, you must understand your partner's purpose for speaking (his motive), as well as his feelings within the message and about it. If you're uncertain about any of it, ask him. You are as responsible for understanding his meaning (even if he doesn't speak it clearly), as he is for sending it correctly.

When you take some of the responsibility for getting your partner's message right, you help him clarify himself and you also help the relationship. Sometimes, you too, need help from him in explaining what you mean. So, support one another. Relationship is a partnership; partners help each other.

Second: Be Present. *** To accomplish your listening task, you must set aside your own needs and wants of the moment so that you are "present" to your partner. You must make him your sole focus, as you will surely need him to do the same for you sometime later. Practice attending.

107

For example, when your partner speaks, don't be absorbed with other thoughts, like evaluating his opinions or thinking about what you will say next. If you're busy shaping responses, you aren't listening. If you aren't listening, you can't get his message. If you don't get his message, you cheat both of you.

If you honestly know that you cannot give him your complete attention at that moment, tell him so and set a time when you can. Then, show up and do it.

Third: Listen for Feelings. *** Strive to hear the feelings behind his words; they are often more important than the words themselves. Don't make assumptions or judgments, and don't jump to conclusions. Listen to him carefully. Ask questions. Get the information you need to accurately interpret your partner's messages. Then, go further: check out your conclusions with him.

If you concentrate your attention, and immerse yourself in his message, you will avoid feeling annoyed or frustrated. You will not have to say, "What was that again? I didn't hear you."

Your Payoff.

This is certain. When you seek awareness about your personal process, you not only invest in yourself, but also in your relationship. Your time and effort pays off, first for you individually (good communication is an undeniable asset, no matter where you use it), and then for your relationship. So, study you; observe yourself and listen to you while you're relating. Then, carefully observe and listen to your partner.

Yes, it's true; because there are many significant layers within each person, talking with one another is a complex and often, delicate process.

෴෴෴

More ideas on creating good communication come in the next chapter. By the time you get there, you will have the

108

preceding ones firmly in mind, and you will have read and absorbed the following concept about disclosure. You'll be ready to take in more ideas. In the meantime, don't forget to practice.

ೞೞೞ

How Much About You Do You Really Disclose: Everything Or Nothing?

We humans speak with each other at different levels, from surface to deep, from zero disclosure to the full openness of "now" intimacy. What follows is a concept about how we each do this talk with others and why. Using this model, you can identify your own disclosure level as you talk.   And, you can see how much others are allowing you to know about themselves. Maybe you've never really thought about this. But, it becomes very important in an intimate relationship.

The five "talk" levels described below go from surface exchange to deep disclosure. As you read, think about why you choose the level you do with certain people, particularly the ones you love most.

1. Greetings.

At this surface talk level, you reveal nothing of yourself nor do you ask anything from the other. Surface dialogue might sound like this.

"Hi, how are you?" "Fine, how are you?" or "Hey, how's it going?" "All right, how about you?" or "Hi Maggie, haven't seen you in awhile." "Nope, you neither, Jim."

None of the speakers invest anything, nor do they expect anything, except what they receive. It's simply a pleasant exchange.

2. Reporting and Gossiping.

A. Reporting About Yourself. *** Family members do this all the time around the breakfast or dinner table.

"Hi, Mom," "Oh hi, Tom, how did your day go?" "Okay, I guess. Well, actually, busy. I've got a ton of homework to do tonight."

"Kathy, what have you been up to all day?" "Well, I didn't get as much done as I planned, just some errands. But, I did talk to your mother. She wants you to call her." "Yeah, sure, I will."

"Jane, I'm using the last of the orange juice here; I'll stop at the store on the way home tonight." "No thanks, I'll do it. I've got a grocery list started, and since I'm taking Lisa to dance class, I'll pick up a few things then."

These exchanges report behavior only. Nothing is spoken about thoughts or feelings, although you can usually hear them or feel them, if you are listening carefully and have your own antenna up.

B. Reporting About Others. *** When a person reports about others simply to give information, it can be helpful. An example:

"Donna, I called to let you know that Mary isn't coming to dinner on Saturday night. She was in a car accident and broke her arm. She's in a lot of pain with it." "Oh, I'm sorry to hear that. When you talk to her again, tell her we'll miss her."

This kind of reporting can be useful and caring. It keeps people connected. The motive behind the talk is positive; the talk itself is clear.

But, let's pause. Even here, good motive or not, Phil may be on unsafe ground. If for some reason, Mary doesn't want Donna to know about her leg, or she wants to tell others about it herself, she could be annoyed or worse with him. Or, if in repeating what he thought he heard, he didn't get it right.

Example:

"Phil, why did you tell Donna that I. . . ?" "Because you said . . ." "No, I didn't! I said . . ." "But, I'm sure you said . . ." And, so on.

This is a pretty familiar experience for most of us, and it's not a good one. That's why it's best to check with the other person to make sure you have the information right, and that it's okay to repeat it. Otherwise, talking about someone else can be risky.

C. Gossiping.

Gossip is a different kind of reporting about others. It's prompted by a different motive. Typically, when we engage in gossip, we're criticizing or judging or revealing secrets. The motive is dark; the "small talk" is meant in some way to harm the person we're talking about, and to create a collusion, an exclusive bond, between the speakers.

Example:

Beth: "Kathy, did you hear what Louise said to Cora the other day? Honestly, Cora was so hurt; she said she won't ever be friendly with Louise again. And, here I am having the whole family over for dinner next month. I'm tempted to leave Louise out. She's so mean; who knows how she'll act if she and Cora are together." Kathy: "Don't invite her. If she can't be nicer, she doesn't deserve to be with us. I've never liked her anyway, even from the day Jack married her."

Now, if gossip poses such potential dangers, why do we do it? There are several probable motives.

1. It could be that, gossiping and sharing opinions about someone else feels like a relationship. Through "small talk" you and the person you talk to create what looks and sounds like a relationship. After all, you are talking about thoughts and feelings. That's a relationship, right? But, wait a minute. No, it isn't a true relationship, even though it looks like one. One of the most important ingredients of intimacy is missing: trust.

True relationship is open, respectful of all, and has positive motives. The person who understands relationship doesn't make judgments. Why not? He understands that he can't know why a person behaves as he does. This idea is

111

correct. Since we can't crawl inside the other person, and think his thoughts or feel his feelings, the best we can do is guess at them. Then, respect demands that we check out our conclusions before we talk about them. So, the finest behavior refuses to engage in gossip.

2. If you gossip, you might do so because it's personally safe for you. The talk is about someone else. You reveal nothing about you. You aren't vulnerable because you shield yourself.

3. If you gossip, it might be because you feel powerful when you know something that the other person doesn't. So, if his face registers surprise or shock or satisfaction when you tell him what you know, you feel a momentary "lift." It's a small payoff, but it could be an important one for you.

Maybe the exact reason why you gossip isn't included here, but you get the idea. Does your behavior come from any of these purposes? Or, others? If you gossip, search inside you for your motive.

More importantly, do you want your intimate relationships to be based on the illusion of closeness, or do you want the real thing? Do you want relationship that is grounded in trust, respect, love, cooperation and mutual sharing? Yes! Then, you'll have to ask yourself, "Do I really want to gossip?"

ॐॐॐ

I'm sad to say that many couples and even whole families go a lifetime connected only by greetings, reporting and gossiping. Each person passes through life without really knowing the others in any deep way. Is this happening to you? I hope not; please don't let it.

Let's go a level deeper.

ॐॐॐ

3. "Head" Talk.

If we decide to disclose more, we expose some of our thoughts, ideas, concepts and opinions. Here we actually share something from our internal selves: our minds.

112

In these exchanges you get to know each other better because you know the thoughts of the other person and he knows yours. So, you have a relationship around shared opinions. If you agree with each other, you feel pleased because the conversation goes well. When each person is open to the other person's view, "head" dialogue is satisfying.

It's even better if both you and your partner know how to "agree to disagree" respectfully, when you have different opinions. The relationship, the respect, along with the good will and love you have for each other, is preserved.

Example:

"Amy, your brother called and was talking about his new home in Florida." "Oh, what did he say about it?" "He says he likes it, but I don't see how he can. It's too humid down there in the summer." "I know what you think about the weather and the crowds there, Joe, and I agree, but I'm glad none of that is spoiling Ken's experience. After all, he doesn't have a choice; that's where his job is." "Yeah, I know. Maybe it'll grow on me if we go down for a visit." "Good, let's start planning that."

But, too often, "head" conversation turns competitive. Opposition arises when you don't share the same opinions, and you each feel protective about your views. Or, one or both of you may own the beliefs, "I'm right," or "I must win." So, neither one opens to the other's perspective. No one acts to nourish the relationship. Instead, being "right" or "winning" emerges as the most important purpose, and when it does, the relationship loses.

Example:

"Amy, your brother called and was talking about his new house in Florida. You know how I hate that place." "Yeah, I know, Joe, but I don't think Ken had a choice; his company just transferred him there." "Why didn't he put up a fight? I told him they were taking advantage of him, and he had to stand up for himself. But, he was too scared. He's just a wimp." "But Joe, I've talked to Ken and he sounds happy. You know; there isn't a

113

perfect place to live. Florida has its drawbacks, but I think overall, he's doing okay with it." "That's right, Amy; take his side. Go ahead; argue with me. That's what you always do when we're talking about your family. You never think I'm right, even on something this simple. Don't expect me to talk to you about your family anymore." "But Joe . . ." "Shut up and leave me alone!"

Yes, "head talk" can acquaint you and your partner with each other's thoughts and opinions. And, this kind of talk is great when it works, but you can see the dangers. Competition in any relationship always creates some level of fear, and gradually, resentment, but it's especially destructive between intimate partners. Why? Eventually, profoundly damaged feelings drives people apart.

Be careful how you use your "head" talk. Decide to put your relationship first. When you exchange thoughts, be honest, but at the same time use language carefully; show respect. Give up any competition. Instead, create emotional safety for your partner. Generate trust. Remember, you love this person.

ào ào ào

Always look deeper for the beliefs and motives that drive your talk.

ào ào ào

4. Feeling Talk.

Deep emotional exchange happens only when you reveal your feelings. Feelings are different from thoughts. Thoughts are safer; many people share the same thoughts at the same time about the same topic. This isn't true of feelings. A person feels a feeling at a moment in time because of what he is experiencing in that instant.

When you share feelings, especially over time, you give the other person continual glimpses of your feeling center. You let him into your heart and your spirit, the most tender parts of

114

you. Your consistent disclosure offers him a deeper, more exclusive recognition of you.

Let's go down to that layer to deeper disclosure.

ॐॐॐ

Each person's feelings are unique. They arise out of the reality of the moment. Others may express disbelief or confusion about your feelings; perhaps they don't understand them. But, they would be incorrect to say you shouldn't have them. Everyone has feelings, even though some people are unaware of which ones they are.

When we want to share feelings, we can talk about feelings from our past, or those that we are experiencing right now.

A. Feeling Talk from the Past.

You can do two kinds of "feeling" talk from your past: (1) feelings from your recent past, perhaps yesterday, or last weekend, (2) feelings from your distant past, perhaps from childhood, or from some   prior relationship, or even from earlier in your current relationship.

Recent Past.

Here's an example of me sharing my feelings from the previous day.

Monday morning I go to work. Once there I call you, my friend in the next office, and ask if we can do lunch together. During the meal, I tell you about an incident that occurred over the weekend. I talk about the details of what happened, and my thoughts about it. And, I also tell you my feelings about it. Since you value our relationship, you're glad that I shared my feelings.   You   know I opened a part of me that I reserve only for someone I trust, and with whom I have a solid relationship.

115

Distant Past.

Here's an example of me sharing my feelings from the distant past.

If you and I are together at lunch one day and the subject of birthday celebrations comes up, I share my memories of my own childhood birthdays, and my feelings about them. While I might acknowledge the facts about those days to many people, I would only disclose my feelings to someone I trust. You the same.

ॐ ॐ ॐ

It might be difficult for you to share feelings at all, trust or not. Why? Because even if you don't realize it consciously, unconsciously you know you're exposed when you reveal your feelings. You're vulnerable and some deep inner part of you knows that being unguarded can be emotionally risky.

Now, ask yourself, how open are you with your intimate partner? Is he free with you about his feelings? Do you trust each other enough to share deeply? If yes, great! If not, why not? What will it take to create enough trust?

ॐ ॐ ॐ

In a marriage that's in trouble, it's common for one person or the other to feel lonely because his partner doesn't receive or reveal feelings. Usually the person not listening or sharing either doesn't know his feelings, or for some reason doesn't want to disclose them. Since sharing feelings is so necessary for true emotional intimacy or even deep friendship, we need some understanding of why it's so difficult to express them. The example that follows offers some insights.

Michelle and Bob.

Married for seventeen years, Michelle and Bob have a good relationship. They admire and support each other in their respective roles, which are work for him and for her, parenting three young children and running the household. They each have good life skills and use them together well. They love each other. Despite these positives, Michelle was depressed.

The "Feeling" Person.

After talking with Michelle briefly, it became clear that she is a "feeling" person. That is, as daily life happens or "comes in" to Michelle, she responds to it from her feeling center first, and then "gets in her head" to sort the information and to solve the problem, if there is one. She experiences her feelings first; then her thoughts form.

If you are this kind of "feeling" person, you are always "in relationship" with others. That is, you are continually aware of others at a feeling level. You're tuned into their feelings, body signals, and thus, often their unspoken wants or needs. There is a sort of invisible connection that you have with others. You are truly "at home" in relationships.

Michelle likes people. She is willing to trust them unless they break her trust. Michelle seeks to understand people, their feelings, their motives and the purposes behind their behaviors. She values people and will invest in them. And, she's open. Once she establishes trust with someone, she reveals herself in correct ways and to appropriate limits. This isn't to say that she reveals all to everyone. No. But, she's comfortable relating to people at various depths. Because she's aware of feelings, Michelle knows when her connection with someone is strong, and also when it's suffering.

The "Head" Person.

Unlike Michelle, Bob is a "head" person. When life happens or "comes in" to him, he responds first from his thinking center, and from there, often goes to solving problems. He doesn't access his feelings. Of course, he has them (feelings live in all of us all of the time, even if we are unaware of them), but often, he doesn't know them. And in fact, Bob doesn't want to know them.

117

If you are a "head" person, you are probably more emotionally distant or withdrawn. You are observant of people rather than "in it," that is, present in relationship with them. This may not be apparent to others because you can seem to be involved with them. You can even be quite charming, particularly in a group. But, that aside, you are not as interested in people, as you are interested in more practical, day-to-day matters. You do not value each person as the "feeling" person does. You may even be skeptical, distrustful, and judgmental of others. You do not have an invisible, positive connection with others, as the "feeling" person usually does. You save that for your immediate family members, particularly your chosen partner. You probably think of yourself as a loner and you like being one.

The Difference.

The difference between these two life postures is enormous. "Feeling" and "head" people not only experience life differently, but they also direct their lives differently. Each of these approaches to living, "feeling" and "head," represents a "life posture" that rarely changes at its foundation. This means that people who have these different "postures" view life and people from different belief systems, and often, though not always, different value systems.

Typically, each of us is unaware that our life response is different in any significant way from others. But indeed, "feeling" and "head" people not only approach but also respond to day-to-day living differently. These different approaches and responses show up more dramatically in deep relationships than anywhere else, although the variations can be important in relationships at any level.

How did Michelle and Bob develop such different views of people?

The Home Atmospheres.

In Michelle's original childhood home, her mother, Anne, used all the levels of communication, including sharing her in-the-moment immediate feelings. She didn't have negative opinions about feelings. To the contrary, she respected her

118

feelings and expressed them well. So, for Michelle, (I) feeling her feelings, (2) labeling them, and (3) talking about them, was a natural process.

Bob, on the other hand, wasn't familiar with any of this. In his original home, Bob's parents taught him through talk and example that feelings are negative. In fact, they believed that feelings were dangerous. After all, they could lead to conflict, depression, anger, and even rage, all kinds of bad things. Even worse than having feelings, though, was expressing them. This could be risky for any number of reasons.

Instead, Bob's parents wanted him to develop his mind, his ability to think, to reason life out.   They didn't want his decisions "muddied" by feelings. So, Bob developed a belief that feelings should never come up, even in a loving relationship.

Okay, how does this contrast between Michelle and Bob play out in daily life? How do each of their beliefs and actions affect the relationship's intimacy or lack of it?

What follows is a routine exchange between Bob, the typical "head" person, and Michelle, the typical "feeler" about an important topic for Michelle.

The Incident.

Michelle has a younger sister, Holly, with whom she yearns to be closer. But, when they talk Holly stays at the surface level with Michelle. Oh, she's cordial but she won't go deeper than the "head" level with Michelle. Since Michelle is a feeling person who wants deeper relationship with those she loves, it's pretty painful not to have it with the little sister she took care of years ago.

Shortly before I met Michelle she had invited Holly to lunch. During the meal, Michelle expressed her sadness that she and Holly weren't closer. Holly responded saying that she liked their relationship the way it was.

Michelle was so hurt. Naturally, she wanted to tell Bob about the conversation; after all, he was her best friend.   But as

119

she began, he said impatiently, "Michelle, listen, you've tried this with her before. It didn't work then, either. Put it to bed." She tried telling him her feelings, "But Bob, this is my sister. I love her and I'm really sad about the distance between us." As his anger rose, he said, "Holly isn't worth this trouble. You've been a fool about her. Let go of it." Michelle erupted, "You don't understand at all. I just can't talk to you when I have serious feelings about anything." This was true.

In Michelle's therapy, I had described her feeling center as a pot that is full, half-full, empty, and so on. This idea helped her to understand that she's a "feeling" person, who is usually over-responsible in her relationships. She takes care of others emotionally, and often, physically, intellectually, and financially as well. She gives more than she receives. She often empties her "pot" without realizing it.

To stay healthy, she must choose people for relationship who will give some of the same care back. (One of the core pieces of healthy relationship is this loving exchange.) Michelle wasn't getting much from Bob in the deep emotional area. Because she didn't understand any of this, she slipped into discouragement or depression too often.

Michelle and I had been meeting alone. But, we needed Bob now, so he came in, and we three began to talk.

Bob is a confident, direct man who's in charge of himself. He's friendly and talkative, often charming. His opening remark was amusing. He said, "I understand we need to talk about my feeling pot. I want you to know that, for Michelle, I've tried to look inside it, but I can't. The lid on my pot is closed tight, and it's gonna be awfully hard to get it open. My hinges are rusted and I don't think they'll work anymore." Loosely translated, that meant, "I don't want to deal with my feelings."

But, when I asked him if he was happy with the way he had handled the "Holly" issue with Michelle, his answer was "No." To the contrary, he realized he'd hurt her.

Yes, he had hurt her. She closed up when he insisted that his view was the "right" one, and then dismissed her feelings. He saw that, but he couldn't understand why. He thought what he said made good sense.

Looking only from his belief system, his response did make sense. He's a "head" person who is very good at analyzing situations and solving problems. Michelle had tried to create more intimacy with her sister before. She hadn't had any success. So, from his perspective, why try again? But, looking at it from Michelle's belief system, she knew that she didn't want or need advice, or a solution from him. And, the last thing she wanted to hear was that she was a fool for attempting a closer relationship with her sister. She could decide what she wanted to do.

Instead, she wanted her husband to listen to her; she wanted empathy and understanding from him. She knew that if she expressed her feelings in a welcome atmosphere, she could sort them out and understand them. Then, little by little, she could let them go, and experience the peace she needed.

She also knew that if she didn't talk through the feelings, they would roam around in her feeling center unresolved. She would go on obsessing about Holly's behavior, and she'd continue to feel bad. Michelle wanted her husband's presence and encouragement, not his guidance. Because Bob gave her nothing that helped, she felt cheated.

Looking more closely at Bob, why couldn't he respond better to Michelle? He loves, admires and respects her; generally, they are compatible. Then, why can't he talk deeply with her?

As we know, in Bob's original family home, feelings were never discussed. Even worse, he was taught some myths that I hear routinely. They're common, but they are not true. Nevertheless, relationships suffer from these wrong ideas because people believe them. Here are some of them: (I) you should be afraid of your feelings, (2) you're a weak person, and potentially out-of-control if you give your feelings any attention or weight, (3) if you are a person with "class" or "taste," you don't have feelings, or if you do, you certainly don't talk about them; you should be "above" that, (4) feelings shouldn't be part of any serious discussion or decision. And, so on.

As I thought, Bob owned most of these damaging ideas about feelings. So, we set about dealing with them.

Bob loved his wife, and, bottom-line, he didn't like the idea that he was cheating her emotionally. He wanted to give her the support she needed. He realized too, that he felt comforted when he talked about himself to Michelle. She understood him.

First, Bob worked hard to get acquainted with his feelings. That wasn't easy. He had spent many years closing them off. His old habits made it extra hard to identify and talk about his feelings. But, over time, he succeeded in labeling and speaking about what he felt. Once he could do that, he saw that talking with Michelle patiently and openly brought them closer. The closeness felt good.

So, gradually, Bob replaced his old beliefs and habits with new healthy ones. He gained the talk skills he needed. Their level of intimacy deepened. Little by little, Michelle's depression lifted.

When Michelle married Bob all those years ago, she expected to be able to talk with him about anything. Her expectation was appropriate. Each one of us should expect to share our most important thoughts and deepest feelings with our partners. When each of us commits to another to be in an exclusive arrangement, both of us testify (whether we know it or not) that one of our mutual relationship goals is intimacy. Then, each of us must share deeply to promote this end.

æææ

The Truth About Feelings.

Our feelings are always operating in us, whether we want them to or not, AND whether we actually feel them or not. They are part of the human package, and we don't have a choice about their existence. But, instead of fearing them, or denying that we have them, we can be open to our feelings and make them our friends. Only in this way can we be responsible for our behavior with ourselves and with others.

Try this. Learn to recognize when your feelings rise. Concentrate on actually feeling them. Then, focus on them. Be curious about them. Don't judge or minimize or bury them. Learn to name them. Maybe there are several different ones at one time. Some primary feelings, like fear or hurt, usually hide under anger or frustration. Recognize that all feelings appear for a reason, and ask yourself why. Or, analyze what's happening in the moment that would create them. Perhaps you will need to trace them back to your original beliefs. Remember, feelings come from beliefs. When you do this process, your feelings give you very valuable data about you.

If you use this process, over time you'll put yourself in charge of your feelings. Believe it or not, when you aren't aware of your feelings, they're in control of you and the situation you're in. (Remember, feelings are alive and operating in us, even when we're unaware of them.) On the other hand, if you recognize your feeling and label it, you have the data to make conscious choices about what to do with it. Then, you can direct your behavior smartly rather than reactively. If you'll use this process, you'll rob your feelings of their power to make you confused and defensive. What a relief!

And, there's more. You'll realize other benefits as you practice expressing your feelings. One, when you share your emotions, you prevent physical tension that can gradually over time, damage your body, such as your digestive tract, lungs, circulatory system, muscles, and joints. Tension also weakens your body's ability to resist infections. People who don't express feelings often develop high blood pressure. Two, stating your feelings reduces anxiety. You lower your frustration level when you air your feelings, of course, always with respect for your listener.

Try expressing yourself; with practice, it will come more easily. Gradually, you'll feel better knowing you've done the right thing for you, and for your relationship.

෧෧෧

Recent Situations.

Incidents like Michelle's and Bob's appear in amazing

123

variety. In the following examples the content changes but most of the individual coping processes are the same: competitive and closed. That's why there is no satisfying resolution. Feelings often drive the behavior, but the owner is unaware of that. Usually, neither partner knows how to identify his feelings, track them back to his belief center, and get beyond his beliefs and the defenses protecting them. In spite of their lack of awareness, partners want to resolve the content and go on. They just don't know how to talk openly and non-defensively.

Claudia and Ron.

Unknown to Claudia, Ron visits Internet porno sites daily to arouse his sexual feelings and enjoy masturbation. When Claudia discovers this behavior, she feels sick and betrayed. She knows this is a form of cheating on her. She wants him to understand his own feelings as well as hers, and to talk with her about what's happening. She wants them to go through the talking together so they can both get what they want: for him, more sexual excitement, and for her, finding ways to create that sexual excitement within their couple. But, because he sees no harm in what he's doing, he dismisses her, along with her feelings and thoughts.

Clark and Sophie.

Clark just took a job that involves travel to other cities. His wife, Sophie, is afraid that when he's lonely, he'll visit the local bars. He's done it before. This time maybe he won't resist the available women there. She wants her husband to listen to her fears. She wants to understand his needs better, so that they can agree on some plan to reduce his loneliness, and at the same time reassure her while he's away. He counters that she doesn't trust him, and she ought to know he'd never cheat on her. She doesn't believe him (he did cheat in a prior marriage) and wants to talk some more. He won't. They are each off and running in a race to win, instead of a race to understand each other, especially at the feeling level, and resolve the situation.

George and Julie.

George wants to return to graduate school. Since childhood he has had the dream of getting an advanced degree.

When George and Julie married, he willingly dropped out of graduate school to work fulltime.   Now, he wants to return to night school to finish, but he'll need her cooperation and support. Instead of understanding, she sees him as selfish; she shuts down their talk.

Rudy and Hannah.

Rudy and Hannah have two children.   He wants one more. She says she's finished with making a family, and refuses to talk about having another child.   He feels resentful and betrayed that she won't at least hear him out. He reasons that they have enough money, and even though she's a stay-at-home mom, he would happily anticipate helping with a new baby.   He wonders; why does he have to convince her? After all, she knew he wanted a larger family before they married.

John and Anne.

John's the only breadwinner in the family. He and Anne have three children. Anne is a stay-at-home mom. They both agree that they need a larger house. So, John is anxious to save money for the house, and for their kid's college years. Anne doesn't have the desire or the skill to save money.   So, she dismisses John's concerns and spends as she wishes. She has her own credit cards so she can act out her belief that, "if I want something, I can go buy it." She leaves it to him to pay the bills.

Sam and Amy.

Sam is talkative and charming when he's at work. At home he's quiet, and doesn't share much with Amy or their kids. Amy has seen this inconsistent behavior for a long time. She's worried that his provocative teasing with the women at work will lead to something more away from work. He denies that anything has, is now, or ever will "go on with another woman." He won't talk about it, and when he's confronted, he behaves very defensively. His closed attitude convinces her more than ever that he's concealing something. She's hurt and angry.

And, we could go on, with couple after couple and situation after situation.

125

These problems needn't overwhelm a committed relationship, but partners need a positive process for dealing with them. Shutting down doesn't work. So, what will?

A New Process.

First, speak to your partner. Then, you must "hear" your partner. "Hearing" means that you open to take in, and understand your partner's feelings and the meaning of his words. Second, together sort through each individual need and want that threatens the partnership. Without this cooperation, the damage to your connection may be irreparable. Third, negotiate to some compromise that works for both of you. Then, try the compromise. Fourth, recognize that your life together is a process. Understand that if the compromise you've reached doesn't work for both of you, you can and should admit that to each other. Then, sit down, talk again, and reach another compromise. Try again. Repeat: life is a process. Partners continue working together to get it right.

You can see how necessary "feeling" talk is in clearing the air, creating trust, and setting the stage for cooperative problem-solving with each other's needs in mind. Start now to understand this process and acquire these skills. If all of this is new for you, it will feel awkward, and even unnatural for a time, but building these new relationship muscles will pay off. I promise.

ತೀ ತೀ ತೀ

Let's go to the deepest disclosure level. When you reach this, you're home.

5. "Feeling" Talk NOW.

The deepest exchange between two people happens as you share the feelings that you are feeling in the present moment, now.

Examples:

"I love you." "I'm so glad you came, it's great to see you."

"I resent it when you don't keep your promises." Or, "I'm bored when you talk about business every day."

Simply, this talk tells feelings that are being felt right this minute. If you're feeling hurt, embarrassed, resentful, joyful, loving, you tell your partner as you're feeling it, or soon after. If your partner is feeling loving, contented, peaceful, angry, humiliated, he tells you.

One more thing. This openness creates more closeness when you each take responsibility for your feelings, and don't blame your partner for them. To do so, you would say to your partner, "I feel hurt when you do that," instead of "You hurt my feelings." Or, "I'm getting angry," rather than "You're making me angry."

"I" sentences accomplish two things: (I) You declare yourself the owner of the feeling; (2) You're not accusing your partner. Instead, you are saying what you want your partner to know.

Mutual sharing of feelings encourages both of you to feel safe revealing yourselves to one another. If I'm your partner, you know that I share myself at that level only with those people I love and deeply trust. I trust you because I know you'll give me time, attention and understanding. Then, I know how special it is when you share who you are with me. It's open. It's honest. You know I'll give you the time, attention, and understanding you need to continue trusting me. In this atmosphere, intimacy thrives and deepens.

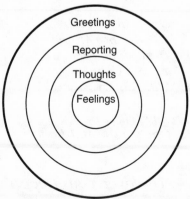

ॐॐॐ

Think about it. Now that you know more, what level of disclosure do you choose with others, particularly with your partner?

ॐ   ॐ   ॐ

Big Ideas From Chapter Five.

1. *A description of good communication.*

2. *The Levels of Disclosure.*

    A. *Greetings*
    B. *Reporting and Gossiping:*
       1. *About Self.*
       2. *About Others.*
          a. *Gossip – a definition and description.*
    C. *Head Talk:*
       1. *Positive, Encouraging, Cooperative.*
       2. *Negative, Discouraging, Competitive.*
    D. *Feeling Talk.*
       1. *From the Past:*
          a. *Recent.*
          b. *Distant.*
       2. *Michelle and Bob:*
          a. *"Feeling."*
          b. *"Head."*
          c. *Differences.*
          d. *Parent's Attitudes about Disclosure.*
       3. *Truth about Feelings:*
          a. *Six Couples.*
       4. *Will You Try Now?*

    E. *Feeling Talk Now.*
       1. *Open, respectful, honest.*

Discover Your Deep Talk.

Chapter Six
(A Concept Chapter)

Respect

What Is It?

*R*espect is easily the most important part of any relationship. But, we don't hear or read much about it. Maybe that's because in our culture, we're taught that love reigns over all. Of course, love is important. It seems silly to make that statement. But, I make it because I wouldn't want to be understood as saying you needn't love the person you partner with. Of course, I say again, love is important.

But, here is what I've seen in twenty years as a therapist working with couples. I trust this experience.

A person shows respect because he chooses to from very early in childhood. Here's what I mean.

For any individual, if respecting other human beings is in the original belief system (remember, this fundamental belief core is formed by five years old), that posture toward others remains a lifelong stance. As well, if respecting other people becomes a value in childhood, that posture toward others remains a lifelong stance. We show respect because we must; our core demands that we act it out.

Love is a different thing. Love feelings are fragile. So, if we undercut them with resentment, chronic anger and other negatives, over time, they may die. No, love feelings aren't fickle. But, understand that no matter how strong they are in the "falling in love" stage, they can shrivel up. How? When someone you deeply love feeds you a daily, steady, steady diet of disrespect, hour after hour, day after day, year after year, love feelings wither like lovely red roses on the vine. Those beautiful feelings simply get drummed out of you.

So, what is Respect? Why is it so important?

Getting your mind around the idea of Respect may be difficult. Even though we use the word, actually pinning down what it means seems difficult. I hope defining Respect will make it come alive for you.

Respect.

Literally, the word respect means to honor, esteem, prize and cherish. These words become important when you think about the treatment you give your partner. Or, receive from him.

We can talk about Respect both as a belief and as a value. It can be either or both. For example, let's say you believe that all people have value simply because they exist, simply because they are fellow human beings. There's the belief.

If you also value "treating others with respect," then when you spend your time, your energy and maybe, your money "treating others with respect," you are acting out your value. Your value generates a respectful attitude and feelings in you. These together promote consistent, respectful actions toward others.

Here's what I mean; maybe you've even experienced this. When you're talking with someone, you can feel when that person is treating you with respect. If you tune into your feelings and the other person's body language, you can tell if that person's attitude is open and "for" you, valuing you and valuing what you offer to him. If so, his communication is direct but gentle. It's clear. It doesn't put you on the spot. It isn't rude. It isn't manipulative. That person gives you respect through his talk and his behavior. You feel it.

Then, do you feel the difference when a person doesn't value you, is not "for" you? Can you feel when you're being treated disrespectfully or even roughly? The communication will often be indirect and confusing. The "talk" may be judgmental or sarcastic. You may feel set up or manipulated. You may feel like a target. People can do this obviously or with subtlety.

Now, we have more of an idea about what respect, the attitude and the behavior, looks like. Think about your attitude toward people in general. What belief do you have about respect? Is respecting others a value for you? Let's see.

Have you listened to yourself when you talk with others? Are you open to them? Do you try to understand them? Do you want to cooperate with others? If so, you likely have a value on respecting them.

Or, are you closed, judgmental or competitive? Are you suspicious, or even distrustful of others? Instead of trying to understand them, are you more interested in pushing your own agenda? When you examine your thoughts, do you find judgment? If so, do you act it out with sarcasm or disdain? If you show disrespect like this, it's likely that you do not have a value on respecting others.

෬෬෬

Whatever your attitude about people generally, that mind-set will dominate your relationship with your partner. In other words, if your attitude toward people is a respectful one, your significant relationship should flourish. But, if it isn't, your relationship will suffer, even though you love your partner very much. Remember, in relationship, respect is crucially important.

෬෬෬

Respecting The One You Love.

Next, let's examine your thoughts about you and your partner, specifically. Try to be introspective here and not just answer yourself in an offhand way.

Do you believe in your partner's intrinsic worth? Do you really value him? Are you "for" your partner? Do you "root" for him in whatever he is doing?

Do you think of your partner as your equal? "Of course, I do," I can hear you thinking, "That's part of love." "No, not necessarily," I say. You can love someone very much but not value him enough to treat him with respect. You know this to be true if you don't have a belief or a value that directs you to do so. On the other hand, you can feel respect for people that you do not love. Respect and love don't always appear together.

Let's look deeper. Let's say you've concluded that you really do feel respect for your partner. Then, do you treat him in respectful ways?

Is your attitude one of gentleness and warmth most of the time? Do you want to cooperate instead of compete with your partner? If so, do you spend time and energy trying to understand him? Do you let him know that you care about his feelings? Generally, do you treat your partner graciously and fairly?

Of course, we neither give nor get this package all of the time, but your positive regard should greet him warmly every time you encounter him. That attitude should infuse and envelop the relationship. If you're answering, "Yes," to these questions, then you not only know about respect but you're using it with your partner.

But, let's consider this for the moment: could you be thinking that you treat your partner respectfully when really, you don't? Could it be that your beliefs, the defenses that guard them, or other values that you own, prevent you from feeling respect for your partner and yet, protect you from knowing that about yourself? Think about it.

If you're not observing yourself, if you are not "present" to yourself, you can't do your part in a smart relationship simply because you lack awareness. Are you being honest with yourself about this idea of respecting your partner? If your answer here is at all uncertain, continue to examine your actions carefully.

And now, what about respect from your partner to you? Does he give you respectful attitudes and behaviors? Have you ever observed him with this idea in mind? How about starting now? You can expect him to know what respect is all about, and to behave in ways that to show it.

ช่∞ช่∞ช่∞

No Respect?

What happens when a relationship lacks respect, especially if the relationship is a significant, committed one? Bad things happen.

When respect is absent, tenderness disappears. Your care about your partner's feelings diminishes, as does his care about yours. Gentleness wanes. Irritation and annoyance hang in the air. Gradually, bickering begins. Heated outbursts occur more frequently. They produce separations that go on for hours or days or even weeks. They feel like they go on forever.

Over time, dark feelings like resentment, distrust, loneliness and bitterness collect and fester. Little by little, you and your partner erect an invisible wall between you. In this quiet turmoil, neither of you knows where the root of the problem is. You don't know how to bridge back to each other.

Where does all this end? In a pool of mutual hopelessness.

Then, sad questions arise: Will this emotional separation ever be over? When? Can you trust him? Can you be open with him? Can you ever really be close again? To be intimate, what do you need from him? Certainly, respect. What else? Listening? True commitment?

What does he need from you? Well, certainly, respect. What else? Explanation? Forgiveness? And, what if that doesn't happen?

You probably already know that when respect isn't present, being together can turn into an awful, awful thing. Relationship suffers profoundly.

෭෨෭෨෭෨

Have Hope.

But, wait. If your intimate relationship is like this now, you can correct it. You can grow healthy beliefs. You can learn new skills and use them. You can develop a new value. You can repair the damage. And, you can reclaim your relationship.

Okay, right now your relationship is less than you want. But, you're committed to learning to love your partner in the right way.

Let's say you've never really focused on what makes up a successful, loving relationship. Now, though, you understand that a deeply satisfying, trusting bond happens: (1) when you know yourself well and, (2) when you focus on open communication and on respecting yourself and your partner. You see that your expression of these starts in your attitude and come through your behavior. These processes richly nourish relationship. You can feel sure that every time you choose respectful actions, you renew your commitment to yourselves, each other and your Relationship.

෭෨෭෨෭෨

Well then, how do you show respect in every day life? Answers to these questions are below; they provide a good start.

Daily Living.

You have many chances every day to show respect for your partner in little ways. The trouble is you may not always recognize these moments as occasions to show him you value him. They are so frequent and ordinary; you might miss them.

Another way to look at respect is that it equals cooperation. Believe it or not, these everyday, routine moments create a lot of tension. This is because partners often compete with each other rather than cooperate. It becomes a game between them as to who can do the least "work." Or, the object of the game becomes "winning," because then that person can feel more powerful.

These incidents might create pressure in your relationship, too, especially if you haven't thought about them as opportunities to nourish your partnership. How do you do with these situations? How does your partner do?

Individual Gifts of Respect.

1. Do you shut off your alarm clock quickly so that it doesn't disturb your sleeping partner? Do you walk lightly, keep the lights off and play the television or radio softly so that your partner can continue to sleep?

2. Do you leave the bathroom in good shape after you've used it, including putting a new roll of tissue paper on the holder, if one is needed? If you share an office, do you reset the copier and put additional paper in it?

3. In the kitchen do you clean up the things you've used and leave the counter clean? Do you remember to replace anything you've used up? Or, do you remember to note it on a grocery list somewhere?

4. Do you pick up in the shared parts of the house, like the living room, the family room, the kitchen, the workout room and so on? Do you keep your part of the house, like your office or your half of your bedroom, clean and orderly?

5. Do you keep your telephone conversations short because your partner might need the phone? Do you give your partner his telephone messages?

6. If you want to eat a bite of something from your partner's meal, do you ask before taking it off his plate?

7. Do you put back the videos and books you use so that your partner doesn't have to hunt to find his favorite?

8. Do you ask to borrow clothing from your partner before you take it from his drawer or closet? Do you ask before you use colognes or perfumes or personal items like combs or deodorants? Do you ask before you go into your partner's wallet or purse?

9. Are you generally ready to leave on time when you go out with your partner? Are you on time coming home at the hour you named? If you can't be, do you phone?

10. When you drive the car, are you mindful of your partner's comfort or do you create fear by driving competitively with other people? And, maybe, screaming at or about them? If you drive your partner's car, do you replace the gas you used? Or, do you leave the tank with less than enough fuel in it?

Gifts of Respectful Communication.

11. Do you wait until your partner is off the telephone before you talk to him?

12. Do you generally say "please" and "thank you?"

13. Do you interrupt your partner when he is talking?

14. Do you resist saying rude things to your partner even when you think he deserves it?

15. Do you look at your partner when he's talking with you? Do you look at your partner when you're talking with him?

16. Do you keep the agreements that you make with him? When you can't, do you amend them before the time arrives to fulfill them?

17. Do you disclose information to others about your partner that you know he'd rather keep private?

18. Are your attitudes and behaviors as pleasant when you're with your partner as they are when you're with your friends? Are you as polite and open with him as you are with them?

19. Do you let your partner know when you come home, when you are leaving, when you're going to bed, when you're going to use the phone and so on?

Gifts to the Relationship.

20. Sometimes as a favor, do you pick up after your partner?

21. Occasionally, do you relieve your partner of a household or outside job that he normally does?

22. Do you use too much of the family's resources: food, income, time, energy, and so on for your own wants? Do you get complaints about that? If so, do you pay any attention to them? Listening would be a good thing to do.

You experience many moments like these every day. Each time you choose to be thoughtful, you say silently, "I respect and love you." You say, "I appreciate you and I want to nurture you and us together." Like frosting on a cake, make it your purpose to top off the love you feel with extra respect.

ôôô

Great Communication.

Okay, you've decided what kind of relationship you want: a loving, full-of-respect one. Then, you must get acquainted with level, horizontal, respectful talk.

Remember, you respect your partner and he respects you. You respect yourself and your partner respects himself. When you both own both of these beliefs and you know good communication, then relationship works. Definitely, strive for this health in all of your relationships. But, especially with your partner, offer this gift to the Relationship. Remind yourself, you love and respect this person. That's why you chose to be with him.

ôôô

In Chapter Five, you saw that you can have a "sort of," but "not-very-close" relationship at the "Greeting," "Reporting," and the "Head Talk" levels. But, you realize now that if you stay there, you won't have the deep emotional closeness you want. For that you need the attitude of respect, an absence of defenses, and "feeling" talk. It's true; you can't have fundamental trust without them.

What follows are the basic ingredients of healthy, smart communication. Choose to embrace these processes now.

1. Be PRESENT.

When you are "present" to your partner, your behavior says, "I commit my time and energy to you, not only when life is calm and we're happy, but also when there's a problem or a crisis in your life. I'm here because I want to be. I'll go through all of life with you."

You can feel and actually see when a person is "present" and when he isn't. Vacant, glazed-over eyes tell when a person is "gone." So can your partner "see" when you are absent. So, concentrate. Focus. Be intent on connecting. Be "with" your partner when he speaks. Your goal is to know him. Your goal is to create trust.

2. Listen NON-Defensively.

When you are on the receiving end of an open, nonjudgmental attitude, you see it and feel it in the other person's caring, understanding expressions. You can express yourself in the same way through encouraging gestures, touching and allowing yourself to be touched, by using an inviting tone of voice and empathetic facial expressions. Do these movements without being sentimental. Do them sincerely because you feel them. In these ways, you invite your partner into your loving space.

Openness is your best ally in relationship. Be OPEN to hear what your partner is saying. Suspend judgment; it devastates togetherness.

You can expect non-defensive listening from your partner, too. In responsible partnering, each of you willingly gives and receives.

3. Listen ACTIVELY.

To listen actively, you must literally suspend your own thoughts and feelings and give yourself over to the task of fully understanding your partner. To do that, watch for any body and voice cues. Focus on understanding the message coming in. To grasp that message: (1) try to identify the feelings your partner is having and sharing, as well as the experiences that he's telling you about, and (2) understand his internal, as well as his external, world.

You, too, can expect deep, active listening from your partner. In a loving relationship, both people give and both receive.

4. INVITE Your Partner.

You receive his information, asking him to explain, clarify, change or affirm anything that you don't understand. You do not judge, assume, guess, remain silent, or do anything else that shuts down talk between you.

Then, it's your turn. Talk with him openly. He receives your information, (just as you did for him), asking you to explain, clarify, change or affirm anything that he doesn't understand. You have a respectful exchange aimed at "getting it clear," understanding it, whatever it is. When you use these processes, you demonstrate your commitment to complete the circle of your relationship. You invest time and energy in each other.

You do NOT compete.

5. Seek to Understand.

Seek to understand the deeper meaning and the symbolism of what your partner is saying, not just the content.

Refrain from problem-solving, unless your partner invites you to do so. Jumping into solutions prematurely usually causes trouble.

If you don't yet know how to listen well (this includes discerning what your partner needs or wants), you may be inclined to give answers quickly. After all, answers are good; they go to the core of a problem. And, better still, you reason, you see it all so clearly. So, you conclude that your answers are the best thing you can offer your partner. Not so.

Your partner can probably solve his own problems. What he wants from you are all of the other processes mentioned here. Why? Because they make him feel valued, taken in and supported while he figures it out for himself. So, stay with him in his thoughts and in his feelings. Let him decide what he needs.

After all of that, if you still think you have a great solution and want to tell him about it, ask him if you can. Tell him you think you have the answer and you'd like to share it. Reassure him that he can refuse if he isn't interested. Mean it. He may not want anything other than to vent.

How about you? When your partner offers you a solution, do you assume he thinks that you can't solve your own problem? You wouldn't be unusual if you did. Most people become defensive in situations where they feel stupid.

Talk to each other in a caring, sympathetic way.

6. Be GENUINE.

Being genuine means that you are openly sincere with others. You are real, authentic. It means that you are comfortable enough with yourself and him that you will risk letting him really know you.

If you want to disclose yourself to your partner openly, practice introspection. You must know your motives, feelings, thoughts, needs and your wants. Then, you can willingly share openly.

Strive to be defenseless with each other, (that's the key), even though it can be very difficult.

Expect genuineness from your partner. Anything else from him promotes suspicion and, gradually, loneliness. These affect trust.

7. Give FEEDBACK.

When your partner speaks, tell him what you understand or don't understand about what he says. When you speak, ask him to tell you what he understands or doesn't understand about what you are saying. Mirroring information, clarifying it, reflecting it back and checking it out all help to prevent misunderstandings between you.

When you respond to him, you give substance to your partner. Responding is a way to empathize with and respect him. When you are "with" him, you focus on what he is feeling, what he is experiencing. When you understand him and can also experience the feelings with him, you achieve one of those wonderful moments of togetherness. You build trust.

Of course, it works the same way from him to you.

8. Be ENCOURAGING.

You genuinely want to support your partner. So, feel and say the supportive and loving things to your partner that you know will help him. Then, remind him that he can use his unique talents and strengths to help himself. Not only is it true, but it will encourage him, too.

Also, you increase the chances that he will reveal himself to you if you encourage him and honestly appreciate his positives.

For yourself, expect encouragement. Tell your partner that you need this. It's often the fuel that runs our motors through each day.

9. Speak in "I" STATEMENTS.

By using "I," you're risking and revealing. But, in a serious, committed relationship, we must emotionally risk and reveal.

Risking might sound like: "I'm worried about us," "I want to talk about something I'm anxious about," or even, "I feel great

141

about this." Partners have been known to hop all over happiness for their own negative reasons.

When you talk about yourself at a deep level, you risk opening a dialogue that could turn negative, (yes, even with the last "I feel great" sentence above). If your partner is competitive or defensive, he might have negative feelings and responses, if you "feel great." But without risk, the relationship not only can't deepen, but also, may be worthless.

Revealing might sound like: "I've felt that way, too," "I've been in that same situation," or "I know that feeling."

In these responses, you reveal your feelings. You know that intimacy seldom happens unless you share yourself.

There is another reason for you to use "I" statements. And, that is to avoid "you" statements. Even though you may not feel accusing, critical, blaming or disrespectful when you use "you" sentences, you may sound that way. Or, even when you do not sound that way, your partner may still feel attacked when the first thing he hears is "you." "You" statements almost always promote defensiveness.

10. Be NATURAL.

Expect these processes to feel strange when you first begin to use them; it's usual to feel awkward when you do something unfamiliar. But, if you will practice, like you do when you're trying to learn any new skill, you'll find that these processes become natural with time. And, what a reward for your efforts!

11. Practice ACCEPTANCE.

Acceptance is both an attitude and a behavior.

You are accepting when you embrace this thought: your partner has a right to his own convictions, just as you do. Your partner has a right to live judgment-free, just as you do.

Now, for you: don't expect that you will be able to show your acceptance all at once. Be patient with yourself.

Acceptance, even for one you love dearly, usually happens gradually as you learn more and more about your partner, as you get acquainted not only with his strengths, but also with his unexpected faults.

If you accept your partner without judgment, you guarantee a future of shared private feelings and thoughts. Why? You become an emotionally safe place for him. Is there a reward for loving your partner and yourself enough to accept him as he is? Yes: one, a feeling of warmth and closeness (that's called intimacy); two, the possibility of his gift of acceptance back to you.

కావకావకావ

If you communicate as I've suggested, your partner will feel esteemed and loved. If your partner follows, you too, will feel esteemed and loved. It will build trust between you. And you will both get what you really want from the relationship: intimacy at all levels.

కావకావకావ

Seeking Trust.

Follow this thinking with me.

If you do not risk being and saying who you are, you cannot get the prize from your risk: acceptance. If you do not feel accepted, you will not trust. If you do not trust, you will not engage in deep communication; you will close off a part of you and keep it secret and hidden from him.

If you are closed, you will not experience intimacy. If you do not experience intimacy, especially with your chosen partner, you remain strangers at some levels (perhaps polite ones, but still strangers). When you live with a stranger, you feel deeply lonely, and eventually, depressed. Is this end worth the emotional safety you've preserved?

కావకావకావ

143

Summary.

Remember, respect means that you value yourself and your partner simply because you both belong to the human family. Each of you sees your own and the other's value. Each of you appreciates and honors the other. Each of you recognizes and wants to preserve your own and your partner's dignity.

It's good to remind yourself daily of your partner's goodness and positive qualities. Look for the integrity in him. Reinforce and affirm what comes from him; appreciate it.

Remind yourself daily of your own inner goodness. Live up to that goodness; use your talents while mining your values. Develop your own positives and then, develop still more.

Life is a process. Through it, keep encouraging yourself and building your strength. Your inner you needs self-confirmation. If you nourish your spirit, in times of hardship it will rise to strengthen you. It will protect you from whatever harm there is from the outside world, as well as whatever harm you would inflict on yourself.

Finally, understand that you are receiving while you are giving. You, too, benefit from these gifts of respect that you offer to your partner. The more you feel and show respect to your partner, the more you deepen your respect for yourself.

Value your partner as you want to be valued.

ๆๆๆ

We've just finished the chapter on Respect, which includes examples of level, respectful communication. I've put examples of the other kind of "talk," the vertical, disrespectful kind in the next chapter. They are included there because, while they are communication examples, (though negative), they are also defenses.

ๆ   ๆ   ๆ

Big Ideas From Chapter Six.

1. *A definition of Respect.*
2. *An observation of what happens when respect is, and is not part of relationship.*
3. *Some examples of Respect in daily living .*
4. *Eleven examples of Great Communication.*
   - A. *Being present.*
   - B. *Listening non-defensively.*
   - C. *Listening actively.*
   - D. *Inviting your partner.*
   - E. *Seeking to understand.*
   - F. *Being genuine.*
   - G. *Giving feedback.*
   - H. *Being encouraging.*
   - I. *Speaking in "I" statements.*
   - J. *Being natural.*
   - K. *Practicing acceptance.*
5. *Remember, trust doesn't grow without respect.*

Adopt a respectful attitude; it feels good.

Can you be alone with yourself? When you are, do you truly like the company you keep in those moments?

 споро   споро   споро

Chapter Seven
(A Concept Chapter)

DEFENSES

The Guards Around Our Beliefs
The Glass Wall Between Us

Defenses: The Glass Wall Between Us.

*A*side from poor communication and disrespectful treatment, the other sure-fire relationship killer is a bag full of defenses just waiting to be poured out. Then, they can smoke up the issue, and thoroughly bewilder your partner. The confusion scuttles him, and puts him at a disadvantage. Then, you have the power in the relationship.

In the world of human behavior, a defense is an automatic REaction to some kind of stress from the outside. When someone challenges our beliefs, we feel stressed. Remember that each person, including you, has a set of beliefs that he, consciously or unconsciously, BELIEVES is true. For each of us, our beliefs are correct. That doesn't mean that they're healthy or that they work for us. But, healthy or not, if someone says or does something that questions our beliefs, we respond with defenses that guard them, even if the challenge contains the truth. We create our own life view. When we use our defenses well, our view remains intact, healthy or not.

Like beliefs, most defenses develop in childhood. Like beliefs, they are an ongoing but mostly unconscious part of your everyday behavior. Usually, you don't even know they're with you, just as ordinarily you aren't conscious of your beliefs.

The belief, conscious or unconscious, guides your behavior. The defense, conscious or unconscious, protects the belief. Why do beliefs need protecting? Remember, once you, the child, decide on a belief, you don't want to give it up. You don't even like to have it challenged. When it's questioned, you pull up a defense to put between you and the challenge so that your belief, healthy or unhealthy, stays strong. That's the purpose of defenses.

When the defenses you use prove to be effective, they go into your defense bag no matter how old you are: 3, 10, 25, or 50. Then, they are hauled out anytime you need them. The defense becomes your "friend," and you use it forevermore for the same mission: to keep you closed to anything that threatens what you believe to be true.

So, we understand that defenses are used to protect unhealthy beliefs. Then, it makes sense that when we find ourselves acting defensively, we should examine our beliefs.

☜☜☜

Healthy.

If you are a healthier person, your beliefs line up with the demands of positive adult living. You are open and use productive behavior. You know many of your beliefs. So, you may understand the motives that drive you. Emotionally responsible people are introspective; they usually have a store of knowledge about their inner selves.

Your good beliefs provide a sturdy inner structure that copes well with stress, frustrations, threats, or conflicts as they arise. For example, when you need to, you ask for outside help, learn a new skill, change an old belief, or work cooperatively to compromise. You believe that it's normal and okay for each of us to have different needs and wants. So, it's essential to come to all situations open, direct and flexible. This approach works for you.

Because your behavior answers adult situations well, it isn't usually challenged, so you don't need defenses.

Less Healthy.

On the other hand, what if you are a person who doesn't know yourself? You aren't introspective; you observe and critique others and their behaviors more than you do your own. You haven't looked at your beliefs, or your motives. So, most of your actions are not only automatic, but you are blind to their deeper meaning. Because of your beliefs and defenses, you do not cope productively with outside or inner stress, frustrations, threats, or conflicts. Instead, you spend energy defending inappropriate and maybe harmful behavior.

Because you aren't introspective, you are probably not acquainted with your feelings. You may not know when you are defensive. Or, maybe you can feel those awful feelings rise and you know that you're defensive, but you don't know why. Not only are you not acquainted with your unconscious beliefs; you don't even know that such things exist. Because you are unaware, you are less successful in life, even though you may be smart and quite talented. Certainly, you have problems in your personal relationships. But, in spite of this, you go along in your routine ways. It doesn't occur to you to choose other different, more positive behaviors.

The Johari Window.

But, why would you continue in destructive ways? A concept called The Johari Window explains it. Two theorists devised this concept some years back to provide: (1) a description of how much a person might know about himself, and (2) how his awareness about himself, or the lack of it, comes through his talk and behavior.

The concept likens a person to a window with four panes. Each pane represents something different about a person's knowledge of self. The size of each pane may expand or contract, depending on the situation the person is in and whom he is with. You'll see what I mean as we go on.

Let's say you are the subject.

1. One pane represents a part of you that you know. And, I, as your partner, know it too, because I see it. Further, we can talk about it freely and openly; you acknowledge these behaviors. This pane may gradually grow as you divulge more personal information, and I treat it tenderly. The trust level between us is likely to increase. Our relationship deepens.

    We'll label this pane: Open.

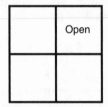

2. A second pane represents a part of you that only you know. I don't know that part; you haven't disclosed it, and I can't see it. For your own reasons, you stay silent and private with this information. Your reasons for not disclosing may be selfless or selfish.

    Selflessly, you might believe that not telling what you feel and think will help someone else. So, you keep quiet because you've decided that's the best way to support or protect the other person.

    Selfishly, you might stay silent to manipulate another person, your partner, or the situation. Perhaps you want an advantage, and you know you can get it, if you don't disclose what you know about yourself.

    Or, you might feel too fearful or too uncertain to expose yourself to others' influences, requests, or criticism. So, you don't; you stay safe, hidden.

We'll call this pane: Private.

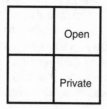

3. A third pane represents a part of you that I know because I see it in action. By consistently hearing your thoughts, observing your actions, and seeing the consequences that come from these, I can draw certain conclusions (not judgments) about your motives.

Your behavior may be difficult, hurtful, irritating, or puzzling for me. When I try to talk with you about it, you refuse outright to acknowledge it. But, the behavior stands as a fact because you acted it out. Why would you react like this? There are two possible reasons. One, you truly do not realize that you're behaving in these ways. You literally won't consciously look at it, and so you cannot let it into your awareness. Or, two, you may actually see and admit your behavior, but cannot concede it's true motive to yourself. You must preserve your image of who you think you are.

We'll call this pane: Blind.

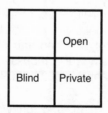

Try not to feel too defensive about this. At one time or another, we are all unaware of negative motives underneath our unhealthy behavior.

But, unfortunately, the truth is: none of us can move from unhealthy to healthy behavior, if we can't admit the truth about ourselves to ourselves. That's the first step toward emotional health: to see yourself as you really are, not who you imagine yourself to be or who you would like to be. Once you've let the reality in about yourself, you have the option to change your behavior if you don't like what you see. You really don't have that choice, if you're locked in a false view of you.

You can see now that when my understanding of myself lines up with my behavior, I'm consistent, whether my beliefs are positive or negative. But, when I talk one way and act another, I'm inconsistent. I may fool myself, and I may fool others sometimes, but sooner or later my partner will catch my inconsistency. At first, he may be puzzled, then confused. If he tries to convince me that I am behaving in a particular way, and I deny it, he may stay with me out of love or necessity or both, but respect and intimacy die over time, because I prove myself to be a hypocrite over and over.

෨෨෨

At this point in your awareness, you may decide that to be responsible to yourself, you must look at you and then, maybe, change. How do you do this?

To deeply know you, observe yourself. Watch your behavior. Ask yourself why it's occurring. If you answer yourself honestly, your answers will reveal your beliefs. Assess them scrupulously. Identify those that you know or even suspect create problems in your life. Especially look for those that are nonproductive or manipulative. Pledge to gradually dilute these, or give them up entirely. When you find beliefs that you like, great. Keep them. Using this process, you will begin to develop a more responsible, happier you.

To go from Blind and unaware, to a more Open, minimally Blind you, you will need desire and energy. We humans often lapse in our commitments, even important ones. But don't worry; if you want to be healthy, you will make it happen.

4. The fourth pane represents the part of you that neither you nor I know. You have beliefs that are buried so deep, they aren't apparent. From time to time you may feel attracted or repelled by something or someone, but you can't explain why. It's this unknown part of you floating up to the surface.

We'll label this pane: Unknown.

Can you become aware of this buried information? Yes, over time through consistent observation and self-confrontation, you can bring up some, if you really want to.

Unknown	Open
Blind	Private

๘๘๘

Now, we leave the definition of defenses and why we believe we need them. Also, we leave The Johari Window, which partially explains sophisticated, and often, surprising denial.

We move to some specific communication techniques, which people use to defend various beliefs. Their owners use these to gain and keep control in their relationships. Because this "talk" is vertical and disrespectful rather than level, it harms relationships over and over. How about your talk; do you use any of the following?

Vertical, Defensive, but Powerful, Talk.

The talk examples that follow show different ways that a person might maintain power over someone else. Since their users seek power, they only feel comfortable in an up/down relationship, a vertical one. The person using this talk unconsciously moves emotionally against and away from his partner. Why? It keeps him safe from intimate exposure and attachment, while at the same time, he can look as though (and tell himself) he's having a relationship. Is he aware of the atmosphere he creates with his up/down talk? Not usually. Sadly, even though it's unhealthy, this kind of talk is pretty common.

But, these examples also qualify as defenses, because they shield their owners from relationship responsibilities, such as good listening and level, respectful talk. They protect beliefs like: "I'm, right," "I know more than you do," "I know what's best for you," "If you do what I tell you to do, we'll get along." So, let's view the vertical samples below as the start of our conversation about the intriguing subject of defensive communication.

Defensiveness is probably the biggest single threat to relationships. But, more often than not, the owner doesn't connect his vertical talk with his own motive of control or his internal posture of superiority. How is it that he wouldn't know? That person isn't observing or listening to himself. He isn't present to himself. He's unaware of his motives and the attitudes they produce. How can this happen? Here's where The Johari Window helps us. Remember the Blind pane and the denial of reality about himself to himself?

Your partner may treat others, especially you, negatively, in very subtle ways. You may not even recognize them, much less think of them as controlling, even though they pull up uncomfortable, angry feelings in you. But, yes, they are anti-relationship because they're disrespectful. So, sharpen up your listening skills.

Also, maybe you use them on other people without realizing you're doing so. Observe yourself. In order to notice if you do, ask yourself: Am I talking down to my partner? Do I unconsciously seek power? Do I want to stay emotionally safe, instead of building a real relationship? Try to be honest when you answer. Become more aware of the meaning of the messages you send out.

Here's an interesting exercise. First, become acquainted with how defensive feelings feel as they rise inside

154

you. Second, observe how long they remain there. Third, notice how much energy you use to defend yourself because of them. If you focus for just one week, seven whole days, on how often this defensive process occurs, I think you'll be surprised. When you really get in touch with this, you'll see how exhausting it is. Then, just think, if you choose, you can direct this same energy to other happier activities.

ॐॐॐॐ

There are, of course, many other ways to talk down to your partner. But, the ones below are the most common ways I've seen.

1. Judge.

Unhealthy Behavior. When I judge you, I decide negative things about you, whether they are actually true or not. Having passed judgment on you, I'm closed to any other information from you that could prove me wrong. I decide that I know the meaning and purpose behind your actions better than you do. I talk to you that way: "You don't know what you're talking about," "You did that on purpose," "I know what you're thinking."

You have the power in the relationship.

Healthy Behavior. If you truly want a loving relationship, you MUST NOT judge. Before you decide what you believe about your partner, you must verify your information with him. Even when it makes you wrong, you should be able to hear the truth. You must be more open.

Positive "talk" examples. To check out your information, you would say, "I think you said ....; is that right?" Or, "I think you did .....for this reason; do I have that right?" This kind of talk is respectful, and joins you with your partner. You already know that makes a healthy relationship.

But, wait a second. What if you are correct in your observations, but when you tell them to your partner, he denies them? He may be back in that Blind part of The Johari Window. He may be denying what you see in his behavior. How do you handle this? DO NOT JUDGE. Continue to observe his actions and, gradually, you'll have earned the right to state an opinion, whether he can see it or not. Why? Because his behavior would have produced a factual behavioral pattern(s) that is rooted in beliefs, like all behavior. He just doesn't know them. Then, you may use your opinion in your relationship as the truth, not a judgment.

2. Send mixed messages.

Unhealthy Behavior. You use a mixed message when you send two or more different, usually contradictory, messages about the same subject. These differing messages are meant to confuse your partner, although you may be unaware that this is your motive.

You have the power.

Matt tells Mary that they don't spend enough time together because she works too much. So, Mary cuts back her work hours to free up some time. Naturally, Mary expects that she and Matt will spend the extra time together. But, when she suggests things they can do together, he won't join her. He sits in front of the TV. She wonders, "What's going on here? Did I get the wrong message?"

Healthy Behavior. Send one message at a time and whatever you say, mean it. Be clear with your partner. If you make a request of him, follow through.

3. Have a hidden agenda.

Unhealthy Behavior. You have a hidden agenda when you have a purpose for your communication or your actions that only you know. Since you have information your partner doesn't, he has no awareness that you have a hidden purpose.

You have the power over your partner.

Healthy Behavior. Don't keep secrets. Reveal all of your information and the motives behind your behavior. Be open. It will make your partner feel safe. If you truly value him, that's exactly what you want.

4. Have temper tantrums. (Yes, grownups of all ages have them, too.)

Unhealthy Active Behavior. When you have a temper tantrum, your purpose is to control your partner, or the situation you're in, or both. You use words, gestures, tone of voice, your status, illogical statements, or even physical power to get your way. At those moments, you don't care about your partner's needs or wants. It's all about you.

Using active movement, you shout, throw things, call names, punch walls, destroy belongings, and hit to get what you want. With this direct approach, the person you're controlling can see your behavior plainly for what it is, unlike when you control indirectly.

Unhealthy Passive Behavior. With passive movement, you have a temper tantrum by manipulating or using body or facial language to make your point. You pout, you sulk, mutter, and generally, act unhappy. You feel heavy resentment, and even deep rage, but you keep these feelings locked up inside you. Nevertheless, your bad feelings radiate through the atmosphere. You do all of this to intimidate or evoke pity to get what you want.

No matter which approach you use, your motive is to control him. You get your wish because your behavior generates anxiety and confuses him, even though you are silent.

Healthy Behavior. Drop the beliefs you have about dominating others, or about competition and getting your way. Healthy relationships don't tolerate control.

Think about this. You can have control, or you can have a good relationship, but you probably can't have them both at the same time. And, if you do, it means your partner is pretty unhealthy because he puts up with it. The relationship won't last for the long run.

Once you recognize your controlling beliefs, dump them. Realize that you don't need temper, silent or loud, to be heard. Using your temper not only threatens your relationships, but also demeans you. Instead of anger, look inside to become aware of your needs and your feelings. Speak about them calmly. If your

157

partner doesn't listen, compose yourself, and then try again, but quietly and respectfully. Commit to value and respect yourself and your partner with your talk.

5. Make assumptions. (Judgment Without The Criticism.)

Unhealthy Behavior. When I assume something about you, I take it for granted without proof. Alone, I decide that it's true. I don't check with you about my information. I assume my conclusions are correct. I speak and act as though they are. In reality, you may be at a much different place than I suppose you are. But, even if I'm wrong, my behavior gives me power over you. Because right or wrong, I behave as though my opinion, view or information is true.

If you protest, I discount you. I treat you as though you cannot be trusted, even though in daily living you may be very reliable. If I hang onto this illusion, though, I have the relationship power for the moment.

Healthy Behavior. Drop any beliefs like, "I know." Understand that you don't know until you've asked for and received the information directly from the source person. In other words, "check out" whatever data you think you know. This shows respect for the other person and promotes trust between you. With this approach, you prove that power isn't your goal; relationship is.

6. Use sarcasm.

Unhealthy Behavior. You subtly (or sometimes not so subtly) ridicule, sneer, mock, show contempt, or tease to send a message to your partner that you don't have the courage to give him directly. So, you do it with "just kidding".

When your partner protests, you say you were just having a little fun. You hope he will "get" the message and agree with you. But you won't risk confrontation. Instead, you deny that your words had any meaning at all, much less a deeper one. You might say, for example, "Oh, I didn't mean anything by that; I was just kidding!" or "Can't you take a joke?" You deny it because, either, (1) you really are not aware of the motive behind your remark, or (2) you do know your motive, but you are not courageous enough to speak about it directly to your partner.

Of course, you have the power; when you use sarcasm, you confuse others.

Healthy Behavior. Direct, respectful communication is always the best because it's clear. It generates trust. You may be afraid to be direct, because you risk being misunderstood, or you risk being attacked. Still, clear talk has to be used so that misunderstandings, or differences of view can be worked out easily. It's the only way true friendship and intimacy can happen.

7. Interrupt.

Unhealthy Behavior. You speak when your partner is speaking. You think that what you have to say is more important. You don't think you have to apologize. You have the power. But, you may not have a real relationship.

Healthy Behavior. You should be too busy focusing on and listening to your partner, to interrupt him. You should be anxious to hear what your partner means, not just what he is saying. You should not be anxious to overwhelm him with what you have to say. Remember that there will always be time to say what you need to. Then, discipline yourself to listen. Your partner will appreciate it. It could make or break the relationship.

8. Chronically Argue or Debate.

Unhealthy Behavior. To everything your partner says or wants or needs, you "argue" by commenting, giving meaningless information, yes-butting, and so on. With these negative behaviors, you create a low-level, but very real, friction and resistance, in nearly every interaction. This chronic struggle produces chronic tension in your partner about you.

When he first notices this, your partner is puzzled. He tries to cope by understanding your needs, and providing them for you. Gradually though, as the process continues, he removes himself from you emotionally. In trying to sort out what you want and get what you mean straight, so as to understand it, he develops a deep perpetual tiredness, and eventually gives up trying to be heard or get his own needs met. Then, the coast is clear for you to get your way all the time. Definitely, you have the power.

Healthy Behavior. Listen actively, with undivided attention, to all messages from your partner. Try to see issues from his point of view, without immediately judging and stereotyping them. Be sensitive to unspoken feelings and thoughts. Then, be prepared to negotiate and compromise on what you want. True, you may give up some of what you want but you get something valuable in exchange: intimacy.

శ్రీశ్రీశ్రీ

As you can see, with all of these negative communications YOU HAVE THE POWER. You do not have a healthy, smart relationship.

శ్రీశ్రీశ్రీ

Defensiveness is not a part of respect and trust. And so, it's not part of a healthy relationship. When defensiveness continues over time, not only does the closeness that you covet not occur; you drift even farther apart from each other. You each become suspicious. You don't share your private thoughts or feelings. You polarize. Because you each see the world from your own unique position, you see your approach to life as the right way—sometimes, as the only way. Because of this attitude, you and your partner become impossibly divided. Over time as your conflicts multiply, living with one another becomes increasingly painful. Your hurt deepens. Your anger mounts. Hostilities escalate and, eventually, you blow. Isn't it time to change this pattern?

If you want to nourish your relationship, drop the vertical talk. Don't try to top your partner. Strive to stay level and equal; it's the only way closeness grows.

శ్రీశ్రీశ్రీ

The ideas that (1) beliefs create behavior and that (2) defenses protect beliefs should be clear now. When the belief is unhealthy, behavior is corrupted right at the foundation. That's difficult enough. But then, when the belief is heavily defended by defensive behaviors that look all right on the surface, it becomes very, very difficult to figure out what's going on. Keep this in mind as you read the next chapter.

ôæ ôæ ôæ

Big Ideas From Chapter Seven.

1. *Definition of Defenses: Behaviors (processes)
    that are used for power.*

2. *Johari's Window: Four Parts.*
    Open
    Private
    Blind
    Unknown

3. *Vertical, Disrespectful Defenses.*

    A. *Judge*
    B. *Mixed Messages*
    C. *Hidden Agenda*
    D. *Temper Tantrums*
    E. *Assumptions*
    F. *Sarcasm*
    G. *Interrupt*
    H. *Chronically Argue or Debate*

    It will be great to be rid of these.

The man who removes a mountain begins by carrying away small stones.

2 2 2

Chapter Eight

Defenses We Act Out

Behavior

*E*arlier I wrote that I find defenses fascinating. I think as you know more about them, you will, too. The ones we've just finished are those that most people recognize. But, the next few chapters introduce unexpected, and often, hard-to-recognize defenses. See if you agree.

Confusion happens because defensive people often speak truthful statements to defend their unhealthy behavior. "Well, if the messages are true," you might ask, "how can they be defenses?" The answer is in the sender's motive. His motive is to justify his behavior, and protect his belief. So, he says something that the listener will accept, whether it applies to the situation or not.

The listener accepts the excuse because the statement is true. Even though the listener may feel that the speaker is "putting one over on him," he can't quite pin down why he has that feeling. He rarely thinks about the speaker's motive; that simply wouldn't occur to the ordinary person. So, the listener doesn't compute that the information really has nothing to do with what's going on between him and the speaker. In other words, he's distracted by the honesty of the message. But, the information being given, while true, is irrelevant; it doesn't have anything to do with what's going on between them. It is simply an excuse for sorry behavior.

It becomes even more confusing when two or more defenses are piled on top of each other. Sorting them out proves to be an interesting exercise.

Here's what I mean. Say I have a belief that "I can do things my way." Then, when I do things my way, and my partner calls me on it, I use a defense or several to protect my belief and justify my behavior.

Chris and Jeanne.

This couple had been married 25 years when this incident occurred.

Chris and Jeanne shared a savings account that they had both contributed to for years. They agreed that when either of them wanted to withdraw money, they would talk with each other first. Further, the bank required both of them to sign for a withdrawal, since it was a joint account. In spite of their personal agreement and the bank's signature requirement, Chris managed to withdraw $19,000.00 without Jeanne knowing.

When Jeanne learned about it, she felt shocked and angry, (1) that he would break their agreement, and (2) that he needed that much money. She confronted him. He didn't respond. (Silence is a passive defense.) She reminded him that the bank required both signatures for withdrawal. To this Chris replied, "No, only one." (Lying is a active defense.)

Later, she called the bank, thinking she must be mistaken about the signatures. She wanted to believe Chris; surely he wouldn't lie about something this important. But, he had lied. The bank did want both signatures. To get the money, he had signed not only his own name but had forged hers as well.

Jeanne confronted him again. Why didn't he tell her he wanted the money so they could talk about it? Chris answered that he needed it quickly. It would have taken too much time to consult her.

Here, yes, the words Chris said to Jeanne were literally true. He was in a hurry and talking to her would have taken time.   But wait, this information doesn't relate to her question. Why didn't he tell her that he needed the money?   Obviously, he didn't tell her because he wanted to keep that a secret.   Even if he hadn't been rushed, he wouldn't have talked with her. His idea was to get the money without her knowing; he didn't want her involved at all.   Of course, that's the last thing that would occur to her.   After all, they had an agreement.   She didn't want to think that he had deliberately, by himself, for himself, broken it. That would hurt too much.   And, it would certainly scare her; $19,000.00 is a lot of money.

Let's back up.   When Chris realized that he needed money, he should have gone to Jeanne and asked for her understanding and help.   He might have gotten the money by partnering with her.   If not, at least then they would have the chance to find a solution they could both accept.   That could have preserved their relationship. Instead, Chris acted as though he had no partner.

That's how Jeanne felt, like she was invisible, like she didn't exist.

In this incident, Chris betrayed both Jeanne and the relationship.   Jeanne had relied on him to keep his word.   She expected him to be honest with her.   After all, that's how good relationships behave.   But, instead, Chris cheated her, then lied about it, then defended both.

Now, she knew it was hopeless.   He'd lied to her for the past 15 or so years. For her it was over. Soon after this incident, Jeanne divorced Chris.   Because he loved her, and valued her as a partner, he was devastated.

As you can see, being able to do things his way was pretty important to Chris.   In the end, it proved more valuable to him than being married to Jeanne.

I knew Jeanne had warned Chris many times throughout their marriage about breaking promises and lying. I asked Chris why he hadn't stopped.   He said he just didn't think she'd ever really put him out.

What a pity that through the years Chris had used yet another defense against responsibility in his relationship with Jeanne: he hadn't listened.

ॐॐॐ

There are a couple of other things to be learned from this example.

The Short and Long Term.

You see that all defenses can be very effective in the short run. That is, they can "work" for their owner in that moment. Look at Chris; he got his $19,000.00 by using silence (a hidden agenda) and lies.

In this marriage and in many relationships, defenses work for quite a time. But eventually, in the long term, they destroy relationship. The consistent broken promises, the deep disappointment that grows into deeper resentment finally kills love. Betrayal after betrayal pushes love out until, there is nothing left but pain.

Doing healthy relationship promotes respect and trust. Defenses tear them down. If you value your partnership, you'll agree that Chris paid a high price to keep his unhealthy belief.

ॐॐॐ

Process.

In this chapter we'll concentrate on process, not content. If you develop a healthy process, that is, a positive way to do relationship with your partner, you'll solve whatever content (problem) that comes up.

Soon you will be more able to identify your own and other's negative behavior. You will recognize unworkable beliefs and defenses more quickly. You will develop positive behavior, and as you do, you'll feel more solid and grounded in your new healthier process. One of your rewards for this effort is the peace that grows inside. This is why we'll spend our time on your process. It's where your emotional health is.

166

ↄ·ↄ·ↄ·

Defenses: The Glass Walls.

As you study the following defenses, you'll see that in the first 10 examples, the owner's intent is to evade responsibility, either passively or actively. But, with the last three defenses the intent shifts. There the owner's purpose is to subdue and punish his partner in a direct, even violent way.

Try to look at each of these defenses from two positions. One, ask yourself if you use the defense. If so, you must own some of the accompanying beliefs, or you wouldn't be defensive. Check in with yourself. If you find ugly beliefs, dilute them little by little or drop them; they destroy relationships.

Two, study the people you are interacting with, and try to identify defensive behavior. That will be challenging, but really interesting. Listening to your feelings will help you know when defenses are in the air. You can also identify defenses by watching for specific behaviors. Many of those are listed below.

ↄ·ↄ·ↄ·

Passive Defenses.

The first six defenses mentioned here are all more passive than active behaviors. In other words, the person using the defense takes no overt action. Symbolically, his behavior either stands still, or backs up. But, passive or not, if you've used these defenses on someone else, or had them used on you, you know that they are extremely effective.

Even though some of the following defenses seem similar in some ways, there are subtle differences between them. As you study your behavior and other's closely, you'll see the variations.

1. **Does Not Listen; Ignores.**

The person who uses this defense has beliefs like:

1. I don't have to listen.
2. I can live in my own world, detached and remote.

167

3. I don't have to partner.
4. I can disrespect others.
5. Other's needs or wants are unimportant.

Brad and Paige were driving home one evening from Brad's parent's home. Their kids, Jason, 5 years old and Joyce, 4 years old, had been playing at their grandparent's home, barefooted. They got into the car that way.

Brad mentioned that he wanted to stop at the grocery store on the way home. Paige agreed; they did need some things. She told the kids to put their shoes on.

At that moment Brad pulled into the store's lot, parked the car, got out, and told the kids that they were going in. He wasn't waiting for shoes. Paige protested; the air was too chilly for bare feet. Too, she would feel embarrassed if the kids went into the store not completely dressed. And to top it off, the store had a policy against bare feet.

Brad ignored Paige; he didn't even acknowledge her. Instead, he opened the back door of the car, and told the kids to get out and go in. Brad walked into the store with them, his back to Paige, who protested all the way. So, Jason and Joyce went into the store minus socks and shoes. Paige went into the store filled with humiliation and embarrassment. Brad went into the store with his ears closed. But, he was in control.

This incident might seem small and insignificant. But Brad had used this <u>PROCESS</u> of "not listening" and "ignoring" over and over for 15 years about all sorts of <u>CONTENT</u>, (subjects), large and small. It was an important moment between Brad and Paige because it symbolized that he couldn't really "hear" her, and probably, she thought, never would.

No, Brad didn't listen; he didn't want to listen. He didn't see anything wrong with not listening, especially to those silly topics that Paige talked about. And, he didn't want to "talk about their communication" any more. "Take me the way I am or leave me," he said.

Paige loved her husband and wanted her marriage. But Brad didn't "get it" that the problem between them was how he treated her, both about minor topics and important ones. After fifteen years of Brad's disrespect, she couldn't stand living any longer with the deepening resentment she felt for him.

Paige and Brad separated shortly after this incident. They subsequently divorced.

Brad's payoffs in this incident were:

1. Satisfaction at getting his way.
2. Power over others.

Brad's sacrifice:

1. The relationship and the satisfaction, friendship, and intimacy that comes with it.

2. Uses Silence.

The person who uses this defense has beliefs like:

1. Life must be comfortable.
2. If I don't commit or participate, I can keep life comfortable.
3. I don't have to do it (whatever it is); someone else will.
4. I can stay safe emotionally, physically, intellectually, sexually, and maybe, financially, if I don't disclose.

Mary Anne and Blake, her husband, had two young girls, ages six and eight. The girls wanted to play soccer on their school teams. Mary Anne agreed; she wanted them to play, too. But, she knew she couldn't get them to all of their practices and games by herself.

When registration time came around, Mary Anne asked Blake if he could help, just with the driving. She would do any other obligations herself. Blake didn't say yes or no. He simply didn't answer. She waited awhile, then asked again, and still, he did not answer. She interpreted his silence as an "okay." After all, she thought, of course their father wants his children to be involved in a good, clean sports program. And further, she reasoned, he would surely say no, if he didn't want the girls to play. So, she went ahead and signed them up.

When the season began, Mary Anne showed Blake the schedule, and asked him which drive times he wanted. Blake quickly stated that he had never agreed to drive at all. Further, he said that he had never agreed that they should even play. Of course, she admitted to herself, he was correct; he hadn't. Shocked, Mary Anne asked why in the world he hadn't told her what he wanted when she asked him originally. He didn't respond.

The person who uses the "silence" defense has enormous relationship control. True, the behavior is passive, and its primary purpose is to control self. However, when you control yourself, you may control the situation, and sometimes, even the others in it, as well. That process is happening here.

Blake has control over Mary Anne and the kids simply by not participating. Because he doesn't join in, initially, she doesn't know how to proceed. If she decides yes, she and the children get what they want. Maybe it's what Blake wants too. But, she doesn't know that because he didn't respond. If Mary Anne decides no, she deprives her girls of the soccer experience, but maybe she pleases Blake. Again, she doesn't know because he didn't answer. Here she decides in favor of her girls. Now that it's done, if Blake doesn't help with the driving, she'll have to withdraw them. She feels bad; what a disappointment for the girls. (Other driving arrangements weren't a possibility; she'd already checked that out.)

And yet, as we know, she can't say that Blake lied in this situation. He didn't. He simply remained silent throughout the entire process. Wow, look at his power.

But, wait. Didn't he lie to Mary Anne by implication when he married her? Here's why I ask that.

An implied promise rests at the core of marriage, or any partnership. Each partner pledges to the other that he will cooperate and work together in all partnership issues. Children's needs and wants qualify as one of those issues.

Later, when I asked Blake if he agreed with the idea of cooperative partnership and shared responsibility, he gave me an answer that surprised me. He said that he felt shoved into marriage twelve years ago and still resented it. I asked how that had happened. He replied that because he and Mary Anne had dated for four years, she took it for granted that they would marry. When she started planning their wedding, he didn't have the courage to tell her that he wasn't interested in marriage. He knew it, but he just couldn't bring himself to say it to her.

So, essentially, Blake's body married Mary Anne, but his mind and heart didn't. He said that he had been resisting the marriage, and all it brought with it, including his children, ever since. Mind you, he loved the girls, but he didn't want the responsibility of a family. He found it too uncomfortable.

Mary Anne was astonished and crushed when she heard him say this. She'd had no idea that he felt as he did. How could she? He'd never spoken about his feelings or thoughts.

The payoffs for Blake are:

1. Independence and freedom. He doesn't join in the idea, the planning, or the work.
2. He has no personal responsibility because for him, there was no commitment.
3. He enjoys the benefits of Mary Anne's emotional, intellectual, physical, and financial responsibility. She handles everything in their marriage.

Blake's sacrifices:

1. He experiences no intimacy because he has no emotional or intellectual connection with Mary Anne or his daughters. You can't have a relationship without participation and care.

ॐॐॐ

An aside: Because her partner will not join with her, Mary Anne gets none of the benefits of partnering, like cooperative planning and responsibility sharing. Blake stays out of it. Instead, she gets all of the work.

Partners, who are active like Mary Anne, often say that if they don't do whatever needs to be done, whether it's physical

171

work, thinking, setting goals, making decisions, and so on, it won't get done. They are correct. Unfortunately, Blake's behavior isn't unusual in extremely passive people.

ক্ষেক্ষেক্ষে

3. Leaves.

The person who uses this defense can "leave" in many ways. He can be physically present but "leave" emotionally or intellectually. He can be physically and intellectually present, but gone emotionally. He can "leave" by removing himself from the room, or he can "leave" by removing himself from the house entirely. Each movement sends the same message, but at a different level.

The person who uses this defense has beliefs like:

1. I must be comfortable at all times.
2. When I control myself, I get what I want.
3. I don't have to deal with reality; I can make my own.
4. I won't risk confrontation.
5. Others shouldn't expect anything from me.

     a. John "leaves" Lisa, his wife, every evening after dinner. That's when he goes into the family room, turns on the television, and sips his scotch and water. He's there for the next three hours.

     It appears that he's present, because he answers Lisa when she talks to him. But, he isn't. In fact, his mind has entered his secret internal world, which is never revealed to Lisa.

     b. Emily can look right at her partner, Jim, and appear to be present as they are talking. She may even nod her head as Jim speaks, but she's not there with him.

     How do we know? Later, when Jim mentions something from their exchange, he understands that she wasn't there. She remembers that they talked, but she can't call up what was said. She "left" somewhere in the middle of it.

172

c. Tony is uncomfortable with any possibility of confrontation. If his wife, Hope, leans in the direction of intensity, he gets scared. If she raises her voice, even mildly, he's out of the room.

d. Mac gets in his car or on his Harley and leaves every time his partner, Joanne, approaches a topic he doesn't want to discuss.

For example, one evening, Joanne asked Mac about their Revocable Living Trust. A week earlier he had had their attorney draw up a Trust document. And, even though it dramatically affects her future, he hadn't consulted her. This evening she just wanted information; that was all, nothing to get upset about. But apparently, he was upset. She didn't see that Harley again until three o'clock the next morning. He knew how to keep her quiet; he left. She didn't ask about the Trust again.

John, Emily, Tony and Mac all have beliefs that make it impossible for them to fulfill relationship needs. They feel <u>hurt</u> or <u>attacked</u> if their partners suggest that they didn't do something they should have, or did do something they shouldn't have. It doesn't matter to them that their partner is speaking the truth. It doesn't matter that their partner's intention is to work it out, not to hurt or attack. It doesn't matter how kindly or gently the partner speaks. They don't see that responsible relationship demands respectful communication as well as negotiation and compromise. No, instead, they focus on the perceived "attack." They feel deep, deep out-of-proportion hurt, and they nurse that hurt along. Feeling great self-pity, they're convinced that they've been mistreated. Why cling to this view? Self-pity is a powerful defense to distract yourself and others from focusing on whatever you've been irresponsible about.

Each of them unconsciously chose not to understand their partner's message. They each chose not to develop a healthier process. And so, they each stay stuck in defensiveness and withdrawal. It's impossible for anyone who has beliefs and defenses like these to really partner.

The principal payoffs for John, Emily, Tony and Mac:

1. They maintain power over their partners and their situations by staying out of the relationship, by refusing to partner. When you are not "in it" with your partner, you can do whatever you want to.
2. They do not have to be accountable.
3. They are safe from failure. If you don't attempt relationship, you can't fail at it. Of course, they're safe from success and intimacy, too.
4. Service. The person who uses this defense usually has a very responsible partner. His partner not only does the emotional relationship work, but often, the physical work of their home, their finances, their social lives, and so on, as well.
5. Relationship Security. Because their partners do commit and are responsible, separating or divorcing isn't an option for a very long time, if ever. They're carried along.

The principal sacrifices this person makes:

1. Initially, respect and trust from his partner.
2. Intimacy. You have to be present and participating in the relationship to get this prize.
3. Over time, he sacrifices her love and sometimes the partnership, as well.

4. **Forgets.**

The person who uses this defense has beliefs like:

1. I don't have to be responsible.
2. I can be passive; I don't have to "get in" the relationship.
3. Others will take care of me.
4. Others will do whatever needs to be done.

Both Diane and her husband, Joe, are professors at one of the local universities. They have two children, Sara, 11, and Josh, 9. This couple is in therapy because Joe is truly physically and emotionally worn out from handling all of the family responsibilities.

Even though Diane schedules things, such as fixing dinner, cleaning up the kitchen, and so on, she usually doesn't show up to do them. When she is asked why not, she replies that she just "forgot."

The truth is that during the bulk of her time, she's doing what she wants to do. Maybe she's writing articles in her head, or planning her next research trip, or thinking about something else. But, she isn't focused on her daily family responsibilities or her partnership; she doesn't believe she has to be. And, she doesn't want to be. I don't mean that she deliberately plots to get out of her family and household obligations. No, she puts them on the calendar. She may even remember them earlier that day. But, then, she "forgets." This happens because she possesses the belief that she doesn't have to be responsible; someone else will do it. And, her husband has been doing it for a long time.

Why does she "forget" rather than use another defense? Forgetting is a defense that's more accepted than some others like ignoring, or just not scheduling. Forgetting usually buys time without a lot of criticism unless, of course, it becomes chronic.

Forgetting is a defense against various responsibilities, perhaps because they are too threatening, but it's more likely to be just because the owner doesn't want to do them.

Diane's payoffs:

　　1. Service. This style pairs up with a responsible and practical, energetic partner, thus saving her time and energy for other things.
　　2. Freedom from commitment.

Diane's sacrifices:

　　1. The respect of her partner.
　　2. Intimacy. Joe has grown too resentful about being taken advantage of to feel affectionate or sexual toward Diane.

5. **Avoids.**

The person who uses this defense wants to avoid various

kinds of responsibilities. This defense is similar to that of "leaving," but less obvious, more subtle.

The person who uses this defense has beliefs like:

1. Life should always be comfortable.
2. If I don't think or talk about this, it will go away.
3. Talking makes problems worse.
4. I must avoid anything that might lead to conflict.
5. Something awful will come from getting "in it."

In Ken's original family of two parents and four boys, the father disciplined harshly. When dad was quiet, the boys knew things were all right. But, when one of them disobeyed, that boy got a few lashes with his dad's belt. Of course, they tried to please him.

Ken is in a relationship with Faith. Faith, a "feeling" person, naturally talks about her thoughts and feelings, good and bad. She wants Ken to do the same. Even though Faith's expectations are reasonable, Ken doesn't like this idea. Anytime he got into "talks" in his original home, something bad happened.

So, when Faith starts a conversation with Ken, he's hesitant. Unless it's a pleasant topic, he'll avoid talking; he's afraid. He'll remark, "I can't talk now," or "I don't feel like talking," or "Why do we have to discuss this?" and so on. Mostly, he just puts her off. Sometimes, he might actually say that he'll talk about it later. But, later rarely comes because Ken is afraid to talk about it at all. Why? When someone he loves "wants to talk to him about something," his old childhood feelings of fear and guilt rise. That's the sort of thing his dad would say just before he punished Ken.

Ken's fearful because he's sure that Faith is going to "give it to him." Or, he feels vaguely guilty. Maybe he's done something he shouldn't have or, who knows, maybe he hasn't done something he should have. Either way, he's "in for it."

Ironically, the conflict that Ken tries so hard to avoid he actually "sets up" with Faith. When he puts her off, initially, she waits patiently. But, when time passes and he doesn't follow through, Faith realizes that Ken isn't going to talk at all. By this time, she's feeling disappointed, confused, betrayed and hostile. So, she acts out her antagonism at being put off; she's even spiteful at times. Look, those are the very behaviors he tried so hard to avoid receiving. So, sadly, his childhood belief is reinforced. He thinks to himself, "See, I knew I'd get it from her, one way or the other." Unfortunately, through this incident, he's focused on her, not his own behavior.

ॐॐॐ

Let's look at the negative cycle: (1) Ken owns the beliefs: "Talking makes problems worse," and "I must avoid all conflict," (2) but then, reality presents a problem, as reality will, (3) fear rises in Ken, (4) he avoids the problem (unfortunately, he also loses the opportunity to develop solutions, and to get a closure, which Faith needs), (5) Faith confronts him because he's avoiding, (6) her confrontation heightens his fear and confirms his original belief that if he talks with Faith, awful things will happen, (7) his inaccurate conclusion reinforces his decision to avoid any future "getting in it" with Faith. The negative cycle continues.

But wait, let's think about this. What Ken doesn't understand yet is that Faith is more angry about his avoiding than she is about the original problem they had. If he had answered Faith's original request to talk, both of them may have been uncomfortable, but through it, they would have worked out their problem. That's the reward for suffering the discomfort. Here, by avoiding Faith, Ken damages the relationship, and still has the original problem to resolve. Then, because he focuses on Faith's anger rather than seeing that his avoiding behavior damages the partnership, he does it all over again. Why? Ken owns a leftover-from-childhood unworkable adult belief. And, probably doesn't know it. Remember Johari's Window?

ॐॐॐ

Ken's payoffs:

1. Time. In buying time, Ken hopes that he won't have to talk at all; then, there's no chance of punishment. Also, he hopes that if enough time goes by, Faith will

forget about it, (whatever it is).
2. Has little responsibility in the relationship.
3. Takes little risk.

Ken sacrifices:

1. The opportunity to experience commitment, cooperation, and satisfying partnering.
2. Respect and trust from his partner.
3. Intimacy.
4. Forward progress for the family.

ॐॐॐ

Facing the Relationship.

When you avoid responsibility because you fear it, you "lose" in several ways. First, you waste precious energy feeling afraid. Second, you can't generate solutions if you're focused on your fear. Third, you can't be a good mate. If you want a healthy partnership, direct your energy to productive exchange with the one you love. Don't spend it on anxiety.

Instead, recognize your fear; face it. Then, acknowledge it, find its source (feelings come from beliefs). Realize that the source, the belief, is unhealthy and challenge it. As you do this inner "challenging" over time, your fear will diminish. As you face your unhealthy belief, and gradually replace it with something better, you break the negative cycle it caused. Now, you have developed the new belief: "I will face my fears, and walk through them." Now, you and your partner can work together to find positive solutions because you've grown a new and better pattern. Instead of being trapped in the old negative cycle, you've established a positive one that gets stronger every time you use it.

In other words, if we face our problems, solutions are found, and life goes on. True, we may experience some discomfort in the "working it out" part. But, life is uncomfortable, and painful, some of the time. To expect anything else goes against what we know of life; it does present difficulties, and sometimes, tragedy. In spite of this, emotional health means we always deal with troubles and yes, tragedies too, positively, even though we may be in pain. Facing reality builds inner strength. Partnering when dealing with reality builds relationship strength.

The huge emotional and practical rewards from this productive approach astound most people, but these results are powerful encouragers. Get going now. Break your old cycles and build new ones.

సాసాసా

6. Plays the Victim.

The person who uses this defense consistently, has beliefs like:

1. Life handed me a raw deal.
2. I should feel sorry for myself.
3. If I feel hurt, I can use that feeling to punish others.
4. No matter what "good" life hands me, it won't matter, because it doesn't make up for the raw deal I got.
5. Someone else should take care of me.

Patrick complains that his wife, Vicky, is "sharp" with him. He pities himself because he has a mean partner. Yes, Vicki does speak "sharply" at times. But, is it because she's a mean person? No, it's because of situations like the following.

Vicky prepares the family's evening meal. As she finishes, she calls Pat and the kids to the table; her voice is pleasant. The kids come; Pat doesn't. She calls him a second time, again patiently. No answer. She calls him a third time. Now, her voice is sharp; she's annoyed. He's ignoring her and that not only feels bad, it's disrespectful, too. He finally does come, but by now he feels mistreated.

Pat focuses on Vicki's raised, impatient voice. Because of it, he's convinced that he's being mistreated. He doesn't acknowledge his earlier rude behavior. Further, he doesn't see that he started the difficulty between them. Because he does not see it, he justifies his position to himself. He feels hurt; his hurt allows him to sink further into his self-pity.

Pat's payoffs:

1. Power to do what he wants, when he wants, as he wants.
2. Service from Vicky without responsibility to her.
3. Special attention.
4. Can view himself as a victim, and feel sorry for himself. And, he may get an extra bonus if his children, extended family members, or friends also pity him (oh, you poor thing, she's really treating you badly).

Pat's sacrifices:

1. Pat sacrifices his own personal growth and the deep satisfaction that can come from partnering; he remains irresponsible.
2. Vicky's respect and trust.
3. Intimacy.
4. Eventually, maybe, the relationship.

෧෧෧

Active Defenses.

Moving from passive defenses to active ones, we have the four behaviors that follow. As you've seen, passive defenses "stand still," or "back up" in relationship. The person who uses active defenses behaves more assertively, but the action is destructive rather than productive.

7. **Chronically Whines and Complains.**

The person who uses this defense has beliefs like:

1. Poor me, I feel sorry for myself and others must, too.
2. Life shortchanged me; I got a raw deal.
3. It (whatever it is), that I get, isn't good enough; I deserve better.
4. I'm helpless.
5. Someone should take care of me.

Todd comes to mind here. He complained chronically in the ten years he and Rebecca were married. He refused to be content. Here's how that would go.

He grumbled to Rebecca that her three girls, ages 9,11 and 12 (this is a blended family), weren't helping enough around the house. He thought they were spoiled.

Rebecca understood Todd's frustration; she, too, thought the girls had an easy ride. She agreed that they should do more. So, Todd made up a list of chores, and the three girls complied.

But, even then, Todd whined about how the girls did the chores, their attitude about doing them, when they did them, and so on. Todd never did acknowledge the good work they did; it was simply never good enough for him. He continued complaining.

On another topic, Todd told Rebecca that he wanted them to entertain more. She thought that would be great. Within a few months Rebecca arranged to have friends at a back-yard barbecue, a wine and cheese evening, a twelve-person sit-down dinner, and a chili-tasting "early dinner" group.

Even though Todd got what he wanted, that didn't stop his complaining. He whined that they don't own a proper sideboard for serving. He didn't get to seat his guests the way he wanted; the groups weren't casual enough; he couldn't relax because he was busy serving, and on and on. You guessed it. In spite of everything Rebecca did to please him, Todd still wasn't happy. That's because his discontent had nothing to do with the things he complained about. He was unhappy because he owned unhealthy beliefs. Dinner couldn't cure what ailed Todd.

Rebecca and the girls gradually realized that no matter what they did, it wouldn't be right and it wouldn't be enough. He couldn't be satisfied.

Todd's payoffs were:

    1. Extra attention.

2. Service.
3. Pity from others. The pity others gave him reinforced his belief that life owed him. The chronic whining expressed his self-pity. He continued the negative circle of pitying himself, complaining to others, and then convincing them to serve him. In this way, he kept himself perpetually dissatisfied and unhappy, but very well taken care of.

Todd's sacrifices:

1. Deep emotional bond with others.
2. His relationship with Rebecca.

8. **Lies.**

The person who uses this defense consistently has beliefs like:

1. Rules don't apply to me; I can make my own.
2. I don't have to acknowledge real world demands.
3. My wants and needs are more important than anyone else's.
4. Not disclosing information is not lying.
5. Lying to avoid conflict is okay; after all, conflict isn't good.
6. Lying to avoid responsibility is okay; I always have a good reason.
7. Lying to myself to justify my lying is okay. (Here we are again in the Blind pane in The Johari's Window.)
8. I have to protect myself from others.

Because Linda often traveled for her job, Mark, her husband, agreed to complete their IRS forms, and write the check for their taxes. Since she had given the form to Mark signed and ready, Linda assumed that task was done.

One day about a year and a half later, a shocked Linda discovered that $13,000.00 had disappeared from their joint checking account. The Internal Revenue Bureau had taken it.

In tracking down the money, Linda discovered that Mark had not filed their taxes, even though he said he had. Further, the IRS had notified them several times throughout the next year that they owed, not only the original taxes, but also interest and late penalties. Linda knew nothing about the warnings. Mark knew because he had intercepted the IRS notices, but he did nothing about them.

Mark lied to Linda in two ways.

Mark lied directly when he said he would take care of their tax filing. The truth was that he never intended to take care of it; he didn't want to. Because Mark and Linda both earned high incomes, they paid high taxes. Mark resented giving so much money to the IRS. He decided to make his own rules about his taxes.

Mark lied to Linda indirectly when he concealed the notices of nonpayment, and the warnings of penalties.

These behaviors, even though they do not make objective, rational sense, felt "right" to Mark. This is true for all of us: our adult actions feel correct, even though they come from unhealthy childhood beliefs. As you know, we can even rationalize our actions to fit our reality rather than face our belief and give it up.

Mark's payoffs:

1. Freedom to do exactly what he wants.
2. Control brought him comfort.
3. Excitement generated by going against the rules, and, for awhile, "getting away with it."
4. Avoids commitment, and the responsibility that goes with it.

Mark's sacrifices:

1. Linda's trust. It just doesn't exist when a partner lies.
2. Linda's respect.
3. Intimacy. If Linda can't trust and respect, she won't/can't be intimate. Most people feel this way.

183

9. **Makes excuses.**

The person who uses this defense consistently has beliefs like:

1. I don't have to be responsible.
2. Someone else will do it.
3. I can do it (whatever it is), if and when I choose.
4. I have to defend myself.

Phil and Mary decided to take their two young children on a family vacation. In talking, they narrowed their choices to two possibilities, San Diego or Seattle. They each agreed to research one location. Together, they would decide where to go when they talked two weeks later.

Fourteen days later Phil was ready to talk. Mary wasn't. Phil felt frustrated, as he does so much of the time trying to collaborate with Mary. As they talked, she said, "Yes, I know I should have done it, but I've had so much to do; I just couldn't think about it. It seems like a really huge job, and I haven't had time." "Why didn't you call a travel agency, or go to the library for help?" Phil asked. "Well, I guess I was just busy with the kids." Phil interjected, "I could have helped, if I'd known." "Yeah, but I didn't think about talking to you," she replied. This is typical Mary, making her standard excuses. Why are they also defenses? They are used to justify her lack of responsibility and protect her faulty beliefs.

Further, even though her statements are all factually true, they don't answer the meaning of Phil's questions. (He meant that she could have done something positive rather than nothing at all.) She uses communication here to confuse Phil.

Does she recognize these patterns in herself? Yes, it turns out, she does. Then, why do it if it's always going to create a problem between her and Phil? Her answer: It's easier in the moment to promise something to her partner than it is to say "no" to him. This is true even if she knows that she doesn't intend to do what she has promised. Why? She's afraid that if she is honest, and says that she doesn't want to do it, (whatever it is), there will be an argument. She's a Comfort person who doesn't want conflict. So, honesty is not an option in a tight place like this. The alternative is for her to agree, and then, excuse herself later. That way, she gets out of the work. And, at the same time, she avoids an argument.

Could Mary become more responsible? Yes, but to do that she would need to learn how to manage her time and energy; she is missing these skills. Developing the skills would be work. Work isn't something Mary will quickly embrace. Remember; she's a Comfort style who wants life to feel good moment to moment. She doesn't plan for the future.

To solve their vacation problem, Phil did what he always does. He did the research, decided where they would go, and made the arrangements. This responsibility process is one of his silently implied jobs in the marriage. And looking deeper, this incident is symbolic of the entire marriage. Anytime there's work to be done or a decision to be made, Phil does it.

Mary's payoffs:

1. Service; Phil does the work.
2. No risk because she takes no responsibility. If you aren't doing the action, you aren't likely to be criticized. Instead, Phil takes the risk. As he openly and actively does the work, Mary watches. She, from her observer position, can criticize anything that he decides. In other words, Mary's passivity keeps her from action, and at the same time, gives her substantial passive power in the relationship.
3. Sympathy. If Phil decides not to be trapped into doing the work of making the family decisions, but, instead, holds Mary accountable for her original agreement, she can accuse him of being mean and controlling. She can see herself as his "victim" by convincing herself, and others, (their children) if she needs to, that she really couldn't do the task. She can say then (and believe) that Phil was unfairly expecting too much from her. Look at the sympathy that's possible here from outside observers.

Mary's sacrifices:

1. Phil's respect and trust.

2. *Intimacy.* Phil won't engage emotionally or sexually with Mary. He doesn't trust or respect her; she has been playing this game for a long time.

3. *Phil's hope for true relationship.* They've been married for 18 years but real partnering hasn't happened yet.

10. Deflects: Changes the Subject.

The person who uses this defense consistently has beliefs like:

1. I need control.
2. My feelings, thoughts, needs and wants are more important than other's.
3. I won't listen.
4. I don't have to deal with what others want, whatever it is.

Kevin and Kelsey were talking in the kitchen. Kelsey said, "I was thinking about how much money we'll need to set aside for our Christmas vacation." Kevin replied, "I talked to your dad yesterday about that garage project we want done." Kelsey thinks, "What does talking to my dad have to do with our vacation?" She wonders, "Didn't he hear me?" She's confused and annoyed.

One night Kelsey asked, "Kevin, I just bought this dress today; what do you think of it?" Kevin replies, "Uh, will you come and help me with this?" Now, she's definitely thrown off-guard. What in the world is going on?

Kevin often changes the subject instead of responding; it leaves Kelsey frustrated. "Isn't he listening to me?" She wonders. Then, she decides, "No, he isn't." This realization triggers helpless feelings in her. And, she's suspicious of him: "Why can't he be direct? He must be hiding something," she thinks. Maybe her leap from confusion to "he must be hiding something" seems drastic, but his indirectness promotes her distrust. It seems to her that he's always sidestepping.

Kevin's payoffs:

1. Being in control; he redirects the conversation.

2. Maintains emotional distance. He doesn't address her concerns or respond to her feelings or thoughts.

Kevin's sacrifices:

1. Trust. He's traded it for control and emotional distance.
2. Intimacy. Kelsey can't be close emotionally or sexually when she feels confused and suspicious.

෨෨෨

Aggressive Defenses.

These last three behaviors are not just active; they're aggressive and destructive. They directly attack others. They shove their partners away emotionally; maintaining real relationship becomes impossible.

11. Criticizes Others.

The person who uses this defense consistently has beliefs like:

1. I'm right.
2. It's my right, even my duty, to tell others what to feel or think or how to behave.
3. Others should not dispute me.

The critical person speaks: "Where did you get this awful thing?" "You're a fool if you don't know (whatever it is)." "Anybody can do that; what's wrong with you?" "Didn't you comb your hair this morning?" "That color looks terrible on you."

Ellen is chronically impatient with her husband, Joe. When she can't find her work-binder, Joe gets the blame for misplacing it. When Ellen's reading glasses aren't where they should be, she's certain that Joe has done something with them. It couldn't be that she has misplaced them. If Joe fixes something she doesn't like for dinner, Ellen's convinced he never really thinks after all; he should have known what she wanted. In other words, she uses criticism to stay on top of him emotionally, in a power position.

Greg controls his partner, Anne, by telling her that she is weak and useless. Sometimes he sends his message directly and cruelly when they're alone, "You're so stupid about money. Come to think of it, you're just plain stupid." Or, when they're out with other people, he comments cleverly, but just as cruelly, "Keep trying, dear (as he looks down his nose at her); one of these days, maybe you'll be able to handle money."

Greg's Payoffs:

> *1.* Submission of his partner.
> *2.* Control, and thus, power.
> *3.* Feels superior.

Greg's Sacrifices:

> Partner's:
>
> *1.* Trust.
> *2.* Respect
> *3.* Friendship and intimacy.

The constantly critical person gives up real relationship at most levels, including sexual intimacy unless he forces it. The partner owning these attitudes and using these behaviors hurts and humiliates his partner over and over and over. All this time, the partner collects overwhelming resentment.

12. **Verbally Abuses Others.**

The person who uses this defense consistently has beliefs like:

> *1.* I'm right.
> *2.* I don't have to respect others.
> *3.* It's my right to control other people.
> *4.* Others should not dispute me.
> *5.* When others don't obey me, I can seek revenge.
> *6.* It's your fault if I: (a) talk at you continually, (b) call you names, (c) scream at you, (d) make fun of you.

These are typical examples of how the verbally abusive person speaks to his partner: "You're nothing;" "Nobody likes or wants you," "You're a failure," "You never were any good," and so on.

The verbally abusive person uses name-calling as one of his prime weapons: stupid, fool, bitch, sloppy, jerk, dummy, fatty, ugly, moron, thick, numbskull, dense, asshole (and worse).

The following are typical behaviors used by the verbally abusive person against his partner: sneering, smirking, comparing, shaking a fist or finger, pointing, staring aggressively, yelling, screaming, preaching, lecturing, ordering and so on.

The verbal abuser's payoffs:

1. Partner's submission.
2. Control.
3. Feels emotionally, intellectually and physically powerful.

The verbal abuser's prices:

1. No relationship.
2. Loneliness, no connectedness, emotional separation from people, depression.

13. **Physically Abuses Others.**

The person who uses this defense consistently has beliefs like:

1. I can do life the way I want.
2. I distrust, and often hate, others.
3. I can use others.
4. I can punish others.
5. I can do whatever is necessary to achieve obedience from others.
6. I answer to no one for my actions.

The physically abusive person owns the verbally abusive person's beliefs, plus those above. When he can't verbally achieve control, he escalates to physical abuse to get what he wants.

He has little self-discipline. He owns few beliefs that establish inner boundaries or prohibitions. Without beliefs that direct him to control his behaviors, he can use unhampered aggression.

Typical behaviors the physically abusive person uses are: hitting walls, doors or people, throwing objects. Pushing, poking, pinching, slapping, scratching, biting, beating, twisting arms, pulling hair, and kicking his partner. This person also believes that it's fine to use weapons such as belts, tree switches, coat hangers, hot irons, lighted cigarettes and other objects against his partner to get what he wants. In the following example, both people use fists.

Susan and Mickey.

Susan and Mick, married seven years, have two small children, Amanda, a six-year-old first grader, and Joey, who is just barely three. Susan and Mick love each other. But, they are both intense people, whose feelings run high. They have a history of arguing and fighting.

That evening Susan and Mick planned to take Amanda and Joey out for a quick dinner and then drop them at the sitter's home. They were going bowling. Susan and Mick got all the way through ordering dinner before they started arguing. Whatever it was about, it wasn't important. Arguing was simply how they knew to relate.

Dinner came; the kids ate, heads down. Susan didn't eat. Instead, she got up, walked out to the car and sat waiting. Mick took his good old sweet time eating and paying for dinner. He and the kids strolled out to find Susan furiously tapping her foot.

Mick buckled Amanda and Joey into their car seats. They drove off, Susan in the driver's seat.

Cold silence filled the air. After Susan delivered the kids, she drove home. She wasn't going to go anywhere with Mick; he always managed to spoil any good time they ever planned. He was a first-class jerk and she really had a hard time remembering why she'd married him.

Mick followed Susan into the house. He had to make her listen to him. Why? He didn't know; he just did, that was all. And, he also knew this: he would make sure that she didn't have the last word. She always had her mouth open, yapping. That's why she couldn't hear him.

The minute they got into the house, Susan started yelling at him. He told her to shut up but she just kept at it.

He crossed the room, intending to look her in the eye and get her attention before he spoke to her.

All of a sudden, she moved close to him, pulled her arm back and swung at him. Her fist caught him full force on his nose. Shocked, he hit her back, then grabbed her arms and held them behind her, talking as he moved, trying to calm her, trying to handle his own surprise. She, yelling at him, sunk her teeth into his shoulder. In pain he let go of her.

Running down the hall, she entered their bedroom, locked the door against him and pushed a small table in front of it. She grabbed the phone.

Screaming that he'd be sorry he had attacked her, Susan dialed 911. Mick could hear her as she talked to the police dispatcher. He knew he should leave. They had been down this road before and he knew where it led. But, he couldn't leave. She had the car keys with her. Okay, then he'd walk. But, as he opened the front door, a police car pulled up.

After more screaming accusations from Susan and stop and start explanations from Mick, a second police car pulled up. The policemen handcuffed both of them. One took Susan to the town jail, the other took Mick to the jail in the next town. (In domestic disputes, the policy dictated that police jail <u>all</u> participants, since they really couldn't say who initiated the problem.)

This scene took place on a Friday night. I heard about it when Susan showed up the next morning for her 10:30 a.m. appointment. She had come straight from jail. The police released Mick a half hour later. He went from jail to pick up the kids and take them home.

This happening wasn't unusual. They had quite a list of domestic violence calls on their police records down at City Hall.

You, Reader, can draw your own conclusions about how much trust Susan and Mick felt for each other, and how much *real* intimacy they shared.

The physical abuser's payoffs:

1. Control.
2. Obedience.
3. Feelings of supreme authority.

The physical abuser's prices:

1. Relationship.
2. Emotional isolation and, in extreme cases, physical isolation. Depression. In extreme cases, progression to a worsening social and mental state.

৵৵৵

Looking back over this list, you could get discouraged. But, please don't. Enlightenment, change and healing are what this book is all about. Until you identify the roots of your problems, you can't do anything about them; you have no choices. Once you know why your behavior occurs, you can help yourself and your partner to create better lives. You do have choices. Use your new awareness and expanded courage to tackle and defeat your defenses.

৵৵৵

The next two chapters present information on two more kinds of defenses. Read on and see why they deserve separate treatment.

৵   ৵   ৵

Big Ideas From Chapter Eight.

1. *Defenses come in many shapes and sizes, in different levels of clarity and subtlety.*

A person with Passive defenses:

> *Doesn't Listen.*
> *Uses Silence.*
> *Leaves.*
> *Forgets.*
> *Avoids.*
> *Plays the Victim.*

A person with Assertive defenses:

> *Chronically Whines and Complains.*
> *Lies.*
> *Makes Excuses.*
> *Deflects: Changes the Subject.*

A person with Aggressive defenses:

> *Criticizes Others.*
> *Verbally Abuses Others.*
> *Physically Abuses Others.*

2. *You can dump these behaviors if you decide to. Try it.*

You Can Do This.

*The road to peace, success and happiness is
always under construction.*

ॐ   ॐ   ॐ

Chapter Nine

Blame

*D*o you know anybody who believes he's a victim of life? You know what I mean. Someone who thinks his going-nowhere career is only because his boss doesn't like him. Or, someone who thinks that she has no dates because none of the men she meets can handle her. Or, someone who thinks his money problems exist because his parents didn't teach him how to handle his money. And so on.

We know, of course, that someone who isn't going anywhere in his career might have blown opportunities to "show his stuff." He could look at himself now, reassess his behavior and try again. We know that someone who has no dates might be cold or aggressive. She could acknowledge any negative traits and do something about them. We know that childhood happened a long time ago, and that an adult who has money problems can learn to budget NOW.

Many of us blame someone or something else for the negatives in our lives. It's easier than taking responsibility for ourselves. And, to make it worse, we live in a culture that has taken blaming to new heights. All to avoid responsibility. Where are you with this topic? Do you blame, too?

འའའ

What Is Blame and Why Do We Do It?

When I blame, I hold someone or something else accountable for something I have or have not done. This means that I turn the responsibility for my actions or lack of them away from me. I don't accept it. Instead, I use blame to cope with my anxiety and fear. When I feel those awful feelings, I turn to the momentary relief that blame provides me.

We blame others for a variety of reasons.

First, because we are afraid of risk and change, we look for ways to remain rooted where we are. Blame allows us to stay safe. As we point the finger at others, we cross our arms, dig our heels in, and dare anyone to move us. We may be stuck and feel miserable, but still, we're safe. Blaming protects us.

Second, when I blame someone else, the focus is on that other person instead of on me. So, when I'm irresponsible, if I can shift your expectation of me back to you or onto someone else, it gets me out of a tough situation. True, my benefit might be just a comfortable moment and I may have to "pay up" in the long run, but I'm off the hook right now. And, that's all that counts.

Third, blaming someone else can become a habit. It's certainly easier than doing the "work" of living. You might blame your parents, "They didn't send me to college;" a broken computer, "I couldn't get my report done on time;" your spouse, friends, children and so on, "If it weren't for you, I would have ..." So, you see; blaming is the ultimate refusal and shifting of responsibility.

Do you blame for any of these reasons? Or, for others?

෴෴෴

When do we learn to blame?

This defense, like most, usually forms in childhood. Once you (the child) formed your belief: "I don't have to do it," (whatever "it" is), then you (the child) grew defenses to protect your idea. Blame was one of those defenses.

If you watch and listen carefully, you will recognize the characteristics common to the defensive, blaming person. He feels a high level of self-pity. He's either deeply suspicious or plainly distrustful of others. He chronically complains. The complaining comes from a deep feeling of helplessness, but he wouldn't admit to that, usually because he doesn't realize it. (The Johari Window explains this phenomenal lack of awareness.) Passive behaviors, such as silence and frequent "I don't knows," are strong tip-offs.

(Ironically, the person with these attitudes spends more energy staying out of responsibility than he would if he just faced life, coped with it, and put it behind him.)

Once you know what you're looking for in yourself and others, you'll begin to see how often you or someone you love uses these shifting behaviors. They are powerful.

౷౷౷

Two Incidents of Blaming.

Here are a couple of examples of how the "blame" defense works. In the first story, Tom was asked to do some "homework" for his next session. Our goal for Tom was that he stop calling his partner ugly, hurtful names. To reach this goal, he had to build some inner discipline. To build the inner discipline, he had to practice "catching" himself either in the act or just before he spoke. The whole idea was that he take charge of his talk.

Tom and Beth.

After Tom and Beth sat down, I asked Tom how his "homework" for the week had gone. Even though he'd worked on controlling his language, he still got into it when his temper rose. The names he calls Beth are loathsome.

Of course, it's hard for him to admit to me that he's failed, especially in front of Beth, even though she knows it. He's embarrassed. But, this day he did say that he'd slipped several times. Then, he went on quickly to tell me that the whole thing was Beth's fault. Because she'd "nagged" him, she had "made" him do it.

197

I said, "We've talked about other ways to handle your anger, Tom." He replied, "Well, those are hard when I'm mad." "Yes, it really is hard to make other choices then, but what about the relationship?" His face darkened before he said sarcastically, "Oh yeah, what about her nagging?" "Tom, you know that Beth works on getting her stuff right, just like you work on your language," I said, "We're all responsible for what we say, no matter what anyone else does." His face darkened still more; his body tensed. Abruptly, he stood up and walked across the room. "What do you want me to do, think through every little thing before I say it?" he sneered. "Tom, we both know you don't feel decent about yourself when you do this. You're better than that. And, it hurts you, Beth, and the relationship. There's a lot at stake here. So, yes, I am saying that you'll need to think before you talk." He looked deflated as he came back to sit down. "You're having trouble getting some self-control, aren't you?" I asked. "Yeah, I am. It isn't my strong suit. It's hard," he said. I told him I understood that. It's hard for all of us to let go of an old habit that feels "right," even when the habit is destructive.

∂∂∂

This next incident is more complicated; it has more twists and turns than Tom's straight-line blaming. The example shows why it's so important to know your thoughts and you're feelings. You must be PRESENT.

In this case, Bryan made a promise to his wife, which he broke. The situation exploded when she found out about it and confronted him. Then, instead of simply admitting his error, apologizing for it and correcting the situation, he tried blaming Marilyn.

Marilyn and Bryan.

I could feel the tension between Bryan and Marilyn when they came into my office for their Friday appointment. They had either just argued or were just about to. So, I asked if one of them would tell me what was going on.

Bryan waded in, "Man, is Marilyn mad! I really caught it this morning when she found out that our friend, Marty, and I went to lunch yesterday without her. Now, she's punishing me. I'm telling you; she's got to learn to control that temper of hers. It's crazy the way she just gets a hold of something and chews it to death."

It turned out that Bryan and Marty had met to talk about the three thousand dollars that Marty wanted to borrow from them. Earlier, Bryan had promised Marilyn that he wouldn't talk to Marty without her. Marilyn felt alarmed about lending that much money, even to a friend. She wanted to talk with Marty about it first. After all, that money would come out of their savings. But yesterday, Bryan had gone ahead and met with Marty alone, in spite of his promise to her. And then, to make it worse, he hadn't mentioned it to her. She'd found out about it from Marty's wife, just by accident. "Unbelievable," she spoke up. I could feel the anger rise in her, even though I was sitting across the room.

I called a "time out." "Bryan, did you promise Marilyn that you would include her when you met with Marty?" I asked. "Yes," he said, "I did." I checked again, "Bryan, you told Marilyn that she would meet with you and Marty, right?" "Yes," he said. "Well, then, I don't get it." I asked.

By the way, Bryan is in business for himself; overall, he's a very sharp, responsible person. So, we all knew he hadn't just forgotten.

But, I also knew that Bryan is scared to death of any conflict or even unpleasantness with those he loves. And he has another belief that he shouldn't (can't) say "no" to family or friends.

Bryan knew that if he took Marilyn along to talk with Marty, chances were very high that she would question his request. If she did, Bryan knew he'd feel plenty embarrassed. And, not only would Bryan feel bad, but those questions might stir up bad feelings in Marty, too. And then, on top of all of that, what if Marilyn refused Marty the money? That, he couldn't handle. No, he knew it would be a lot more comfortable if he just met with Marty alone. He gambled that he could get by with it.

So, he went to meet Marty without Marilyn. He hoped that either she wouldn't find out about it, or if she did, she wouldn't be too upset. But, Marilyn did find out and she was more than upset. She felt furious.

When she confronted him, his next defense (though irrational) was to say that their agreement didn't really matter. Finally, he blamed their current argument on her anger. He wanted both Marilyn and me to focus on her temper.

Let's step out of this for a minute and look at it objectively. Here's the reality. Bryan made an agreement with Marilyn. He broke it. She felt hurt, disappointed, and then, angry. These are appropriate feelings. But, Instead of acknowledging Marilyn, admitting his error and correcting it, Bryan discounts her in a couple of ways.

First, he tries to deflect, (a common defense, as you know) by implying that their original agreement was unimportant. This goes nowhere, of course, because Marilyn reminds him that she had made it clear how important it was to her that they see Marty together. Second, when that doesn't work, he focuses on her temper. Here, because he is unable to admit his error (maybe even to himself), he turns it back to Marilyn. All of this happens because, (1) He's terrified of any kind of disagreement or conflict, (2) Bryan fears saying "No," to both Marty and Marilyn.

Actually, Bryan was the one who set up Marilyn's anger by breaking his original agreement with her. In a healthy relationship, once Bryan made the agreement, he would follow through with it. If he didn't want to, he would approach Marilyn to change it or drop it. Here Bryan should have included her, not acted alone. Remember, Marilyn is his chosen life partner. We don't lie to our partners when we want to change agreements. We face them and work out a compromise.

Bryan's blaming didn't work here. Marilyn's feelings of betrayal and anger were justified. Bryan eventually understood that saying one thing and doing another, especially over and over consistently, as he had done, destroys relationship because it destroys trust.

෧෧෧

Solutions.

If you've set your sites on a healthy self and a healthy relationship, you must give up blaming. Nothing good comes to you or your target when you blame. Further, as long as you believe that you can "pin it" on someone or something else, you won't take the responsibility on yourself. With your avoiding, you rob you of an opportunity to grow. You exchange personal power for the comfort of safety.

Blame is something you do instead of being responsible. It's true that responsibility is a burden, and often, difficult; that's the downside. But oh, what sweet rewards, what calm and solidness, grow in you when you take on the responsibility and grow with it; that is the tremendous upside. You can't experience the pluses without the investment. Don't be afraid of it. Try it; it's worth it.

If the prior remarks on blame apply to you, take action now to change that condition. But, let's be honest with ourselves. To be successful you must want to do the following.

1. Recognize that blaming is a passive behavior. If you want success in life, whether in relationships, in your work, with your finances, on your spiritual path or anywhere else, you must get up, get going, act. Take positive action now to form new, healthy beliefs. From those will come new, healthy habits.

2. When someone mentions a lack in your responsibility look at yourself openly. Quiet your first impulse to be defensive. Confront yourself. Introspection is the most powerful growth tool you have in your personal arsenal. Get over the idea that someone, either you or someone else, must be at fault when something goes wrong. The only important things are that you (a) recognize your mistakes, (b) learn from them, and (c) move your own personal ship forward in life with integrity. Assigning fault shouldn't be an option; it takes too much energy, and there's seldom a reward. Adopt a better process.

If your relationships are poor, ask yourself what you are doing or not doing that makes them that way. Take action to change those behaviors. If you're not advancing in your career, ask yourself what you can do to move up. Then, do it. If you have a personal issue, ask yourself if you are learning about it, and using everything you learn to improve. If you are missing a life skill like handling finances, learn the skill. Your life is your responsibility.

Lastly, dedicate yourself to shrinking the Blind area of your own Johari Window. The more you recognize and embrace about you, the more personal power you grow.

3. Learn to "catch yourself" in the act of blaming. Then, stop!

To accomplish this, you must listen to you. You must be present to you continuously. This is good practice because it's the responsible thing to do. Besides that though, you get to know you intimately. And, it develops inner discipline. You'll see. After you get used to it, it feels good; it feels strong.

4. Remember, blame often occurs in relationships because a partner doesn't know what he needs or wants. If you haven't decided what you want or need, you force your partner into deciding for both of you; you default. If the decision makes you unhappy, you may unfairly blame your partner.

Avoid this whole scene. Know what you need and want. Tell your partner about you; it's one of your relationship responsibilities.

5. If you had a parent who modeled blame and you "caught" this disease as a child, see it in yourself and make the decision to dump it. At this point in your adult life, blame can't do anything but hurt you.

Recognize that parents usually do the best they can at any given time with the information and skills they have. Identify the positives that you received from them. Be grateful. Were there negatives from your parents? Yes. As for those, forgive both your parents and yourself and move on.

Realize that you have the power to change yourself as you wish. Ask yourself if you're exercising your inner power or just wallowing in self-pity. How long have you been an adult? Years? That's how long you've had the power to be who you want to be. Maybe you haven't realized it. Embrace change now. Your hurts from childhood are old history, and once you have recognized them, dwelling on them is a waste of your precious adult time and energy. You should be on to your next adventure. You should give yourself this gift of healing.

6. Remember that blaming is an old defense that you have reinforced for many years. It is very powerful. It will not want to be removed. Be vigilant and persistent; determine to drop it.

ৰৈৰৈৰৈ

Being Open Pays Off.

Now, you see that when you and your partner don't understand each other, you have solutions that are better than blaming. Instead, you can each learn to identify your defenses, drop them, be open. Defenses create barriers that make loving each other very difficult. But, without your unhealthy, destructive beliefs and without your defenses protecting them, you can build stronger, closer and smarter relationships.

ৰৈৰৈৰৈ

Extra Thoughts.

Here are a couple more thoughts about defenses. If you have any hope of growing in your intimate relationship, you can't afford them. Defenses may protect you from what you consider to be hurtful stuff from your partner, but if defenses are used

203

consistently, eventually, they destroy relationships just like they destroy you, because they close you off from your partner. They also keep out the affection and love that partners in a smart relationship freely give to one another

On the other hand, if you adopt an open posture, initially it will be scary. You'll be exposed. Yes, it IS scary. But, if you're committed to getting healthy, you must try it. Gradually, you'll understand that you're grownup now (not your small, younger self). You can make the choice to behave in a non-defensive, positive way.

Here's a typical example. Let's say your partner makes a hurtful but truthful comment to you about you. You're tempted, because of old habit, to react, to strike back. Now, because you've decided to be less defensive, you receive his information. It startles you, yes, and it's painful to hear, but ultimately, you'll grow if you open to it.

You don't have to raise your defenses. You can remain neutral. While you listen, you can stay calm, ask questions to clarify and sort information. By maintaining your evenness, you maintain your own self-respect, as well as show respect for him. You do the right thing for you; you do the right thing for your relationship. You stand for optimism and hope.

Your new open posture allows you to take this new-to-you information and work with it. Maybe by now, you realize that this openness doesn't make you less; it makes you more. It makes you solid. You benefit from your new stance and so does your relationship.

The Other Choice.

The bottom line is that if we spent the same energy and time setting personal and relationship goals and achieving them, as we do blaming others or circumstances for our poor situations, the "blame" defense wouldn't exist.

To make life the wonderful journey it can be, I must be willing, even eager, to be responsible for myself. That means I must be prepared to think, (yes, many people don't want to think for themselves), to know my feelings, my thoughts, wants, and needs. I must be clear about my values. I must be willing to learn life skills. I must be willing, no, eager, to be actively engaged in life every day. The only real cure for the "blame" defense is to face your fears, whatever they are, get up, get moving and join the stream of life. Build your own power. Come on; don't be afraid. You can do it.

ক ক ক

Big Ideas From Chapter Nine.

1. *Blame is defined. Why do we do it?*

   A. *We're afraid of risk and change.*
   B. *We don't want responsibility.*
   C. *It's habit, especially if we saw it or heard it in our original homes.*

2. *Two examples.*

   A. *Tom and Beth: Tom's name-calling.*
   B. *Marilyn and Bryan: Bryan broke a promise and then, didn't disclose.*

3. *Solutions.*

   A. *Blaming is passive; become active.*
   B. *Drop your defenses; try openness.*
   C. *"Catch yourself" doing the blaming.*
   D. *Know what you think, need, and want. Speak for it.*
   E. *Forgive your parents if they taught you to blame.*
   F. *Be determined to drop it.*

Last Thoughts:

    Recognize that blaming uses precious energy. Instead, choose to use that energy on (1) valuing your partner and (2) figuring out solutions.

Substitute Personal Power (Self-Confidence) For Manipulation.

Chapter Ten

Pleasing Defenses

The Odd Ones

*I*n the preceding chapters, the data about defenses, applies mostly to the personality styles of Comfort, Control and Superiority. Pleasing persons also use those defenses, but not nearly as frequently as they use the ones coming up here.

If you think back to the defenses discussed in Chapters Seven, Eight, and Nine, you'll remember that the owner uses them to create distance between him and his partner, though he is unaware of this and may, when confronted, even deny it.

People who have unhealthy Comfort, Control and Superiority as their primary types want to protect themselves and their space from other's (including their partners), intrusion. They hope they can keep people and the world's demands separate, maybe even distant, from themselves. (Separate is a important word here.)

But, if you are a Pleaser, you are concerned about only one thing: how to stay attached to the person you love. Everything you do is designed to keep you connected and not allow separation. Therefore, your defenses are different. In some cases, they are the opposite of those you've seen previously.

The unhealthy Pleasing person's defenses look different from the ones you've been reading about. Because of this, you and others who observe you, may have a hard time recognizing them as defensive moves. "What defenses?" you ask. Your behaviors look positive, they produce all kinds of good things and what's more, you do them for someone else. What could be wrong with them?

Here's what is wrong. No matter how good your behavior looks or how much positive comes from it, it's still defensive and unhealthy, and will eventually ruin you and the relationship. That's because your actions come from unhealthy motives and, on top of that, your behaviors are exaggerated.

You, the Pleasing personality type, have a single-minded purpose. You seek to make and maintain a love connection, even at the cost of your own emotional health. That's it, pure and simple. It doesn't occur to you to think about whether the connection is healthy or not. In fact, whether your partner is capable of being a good partner never enters your mind. It's not something you know to think about.

In other words, once you love someone, you desperately strive to stay connected (never mind the quality of the connection), because of the beliefs you own. So imperative is your need that you'll do nearly anything for your partner, without realizing that you may be perpetuating his self-centeredness.

While striving to accomplish what your beliefs dictate, you ignore yourself. Perhaps, you even go without the basics that come with a true relationship, like respect, trust, and receiving back what you have given (a fair exchange). Instead, you settle for poor treatment (maybe you're not even aware of it), because you are so focused on his needs, all the while hoping that the one you love will become responsible in the relationship. You want him to give back, not because you demand it but because he truly wants to, because he loves you as you love him, and because he realizes that healthy relationships are reciprocal, not one-sided.

You don't realize that these dreams exist only in your heart and mind and will likely never come to pass. If you, Pleasing person, accept this single important idea now, the rest of this chapter should help you to understand, to change, and then slowly, to heal.

ৡৡৡৡ

Core Pleasing Beliefs.

I'll list some of the Pleaser's core beliefs, then, discuss them in the examples below.

The beliefs.

1. I need someone to love and/or I need someone to love me.
2. I can trust people.
3. I must feel sorry for others.
4. I can't disappoint others, especially those I love.
5. I am responsible for those I love.
6. Whatever others need, I should supply.
7. I must avoid rejection at all costs.
8. I shouldn't ask for anything for myself.
9. I come last; my needs are unimportant, certainly not as important as others, especially those I love.

Remember, you're driven to accomplish your emotional goal: a love connection. If your tie to the one you love breaks, your anxiety and fear rise to enormous proportions. So, to handle your feelings, you increase your pleasing behaviors even more.

If anyone challenges your exaggerated behaviors or beliefs, you use the defenses you've developed to protect both your beliefs and behaviors. You, the Pleasing person, like all of us, use your defenses routinely all of the time, though usually without knowing it.

The defenses that follow will look somewhat familiar. That's because you've seen most of them in reverse in the preceding chapters.

1. Pleasers Accept Other's Excuses.

You not only accept your partner's behavior but also his

209

excuses for it. Further, you offer those same excuses to other people in defense of him. The excuses ignore your partner's original irresponsibility, but they usually sound good enough to be believed.

Here's an example. I'm your partner. Tonight I should sit down and pay our bills. But, I know that doing it won't feel good. So, I don't pay those bills. Instead, I go to the bowling alley where I can be with my friends.

I can justify my choice to myself and to you, if I need to. Here's how: (1) "I'm really stressed; I need a change in my routine tonight," (2) "It won't matter if we're late with our payment; they expect that," (3) "This is the only time this week that I'll get to go out; I need the relaxation," (4) "You know, these bills are not a big deal." These statements hide my true motive (comfort) and any deep-down feelings of irresponsibility or guilt I might have.

Some of these "rational" statements may be literally correct, but I use them here not because they are the truth, but because I want to avoid responsibility, and because you will probably accept them.

In other words, on the surface, these statements sound okay. They are said once-in-a-while by all of us. But, when your partner habitually responds with them or something similar to avoid responsibility, his motive is an ulterior one. Then, you know he's denying his own motives.

If I, your partner, really believe my own rationalizations, I fool myself. If you believe them, Pleasing partner, I fool you, too.

Remember The Johari Window? In the above example, any excuses fit into my Blind pane when I'm not aware that I'm using the defense of excusing myself. You, the Pleasing person, may be aware that I'm giving an excuse. But, maybe neither one of us is aware of the true unconscious goal (the real reason) for my behavior, a defense: to live life "my way" (instead of living life as it requires), and through avoiding, keep myself comfortable.

Rachel and John.

Let's look at Rachel. Rachel smoothed life's path for her

partner, John, in many ways. Because John drank too much but refused to admit that his drinking was out-of-control, Rachel hovered around him and picked up the pieces when he got himself in trouble, which was often. Take a look at some of the patterns of their lives.

John wouldn't pick up his three children after school on Fridays, so that they could visit him. Rachel did it. She thought the children needed to see their father, at least every other weekend. John wouldn't take care of scheduling routine maintenance on his car. Rachel did it. (She believed him when he said he didn't have the time.) John wouldn't arrange for his own transportation when he couldn't drive his car because it had broken down. Rachel took him to work. "Isn't it too bad," she thought, "that his car always breaks down when he can't afford to have it repaired?" Rachel felt so sorry for John. But, here's the truth. John earned $80,000.00 a year. If he didn't have the money, it was because he drank most of it away.

Because John wouldn't clean or paint his house or arrange to have it done, Rachel did it. It was cluttered and dirty and she thought his kids needed a decent place to live in on the weekends. "Just like a man," Rachel thought, "you really can't expect them to decorate their homes." When John traveled, Rachel took his dog, Buddy, home with her, even though he wasn't housebroken. "And, why shouldn't I," she asked herself, "I love dogs." Yes, but this thinking completely misses the point.

As you can see, Rachel excused John's irresponsible behavior. By doing so, she unconsciously became his caretaker. I can almost hear you ask: "Why?" Don't forget that Rachel, a Pleasing person, loved John. Pleasers feel responsible for anyone they love.

Further, as she silently, gradually slipped into the taking-care-of-him role, she also gave him unspoken permission to take advantage of her. Did she realize this? No, she didn't. But you see, it worked for John because he wanted someone to take care of him. Unconsciously, it worked for Rachel because she needed someone to care for. It was the perfect, but disastrous match.

By the time Rachel finally understood what was going on,

a ten-year pile of pain and fatigue sat squarely on her heart and body. She slowly came to understand, even though she hated to see it, that John was responsible for the constant turmoil in his life. Eventually, she understood that John, at 52 years old, could drop his defenses and the self-pity that drove them. He could be responsible for his life, if he wanted to be.

Gradually, too, Rachel realized that she had encouraged John to take advantage of her. She didn't set limits on her personal resources. She gave it all. So, she was responsible for some of her own pain. Now, she's building strength so that she'll never "take care" of anyone in that old, sick way again.

෴෴෴

A Comment.

Strife and disappointment are part of the fabric of life. They can't be avoided. The person who shuns them denies reality and while he may get a short time-out, he'll eventually have to deal with his current problem or something worse. Rachel's goal of protecting John is a mistaken one. Neither she nor any one else can or should protect him from real life.

The only healthy answer for Rachel, John and all of us, is to take life on. Don't avoid it. Look it in the eye, struggle with it, and move through it. This process builds enormous inner strength. That's what you want.

෴෴෴

2. **Pleasers Over-Explain.**

As a Pleaser, I think it's my job to repeat my message patiently over and over until you, my partner, understand me. If you don't understand me, it must be my fault. Perhaps, I'm not saying it the right way, I'm not saying it softly enough, I'm not saying it sweetly enough, I'm not saying it at the right time and so on. As the Pleaser, I learned a long time ago, that I should keep on trying. That's one of my responsibilities.

It doesn't occur to me that you, as my partner, have an equal responsibility to hear what I'm saying, to be interested enough to ask about it, to give me feedback, to verify the data I give you, and so on. In other words, because of my unconscious belief about relationship, it's okay if you expect certain behaviors from me, but it's not okay for me to expect the same from you. Expecting anything from you might threaten our relationship.

We can see why the over-explaining happens. If we look at the group of beliefs that you, the Pleaser, hold, most of them direct you to take care of other people. The rest of them direct that you should expect little or nothing for yourself. So, your behavior makes sense. Of course, it isn't emotionally healthy to take most or all of the responsibility on yourself, but it makes sense that you would.

3. Pleasers Lie For Their Partners.

The Pleaser's "I should feel sorry for others" belief is important. Because I pity you, my partner, and love you, I can justify lying to others for or about you to protect you.

Remember Rachel and John?   When John was too drunk from drinking the night before, he insisted that Rachel call Sam, his boss, and tell him that John had the flu. She did.

Why? She knew John's boss would fire him if he knew the truth. She couldn't let him lose his job. She unconsciously "knew" that she had to help him preserve his self-image. She was afraid to think about what he'd do if he didn't have that. And, his kids needed the child support his job generated. She couldn't let them down. After all, they counted on her.

Rachel felt so sorry for John. When he talked about his childhood, she could tell what a difficult life he had, with his parent's divorce and all. She couldn't help it. Her love for him got all mixed up with her compulsion to help him, however she could. So, if she fibs for him from time-to-time, what's the harm?

The "I must feel sorry for and protect others" belief really weakens the Pleaser.

4. Pleasers Placate and Appease Your Partner.

You placate or appease your partner, because you feel

driven to calm and reassure him. You give in to him, usually to soften his confusion, irritation or anger. You may also reassure him, thinking that it will encourage him. But usually, all it does is encourage him to shift his responsibility to you.

If you're a Pleaser, you know exactly what this means. If your partner is hurt or angry (it doesn't matter about what), you become fearful and anxious. You're there, trying to calm him. Your job is to "smooth it over" and "keep him happy." So, you do; you provide whatever he needs or wants. It doesn't matter if his request or complaint is reasonable or valid. In fact, it doesn't occur to you to ask yourself if he is being reasonable. Your Pleasing is unthinking and automatic because it comes out of your unconscious beliefs. And it comes out of your love feelings. All you know is that you're driven to "make it right"; you're compelled to take care of him. You must help him avoid hurt and you must avoid any rift between you because that might lead to an emotional and/or physical separation.

Lisa and Joe.

Lisa was a stay-at-home mom with two small pre-school boys. Ted, her former boss, made her an exciting offer, a great job that she could do from home. She loved this idea because she could still be with her little guys, Ben and Toby. Anticipating the extra money Lisa's new job would generate, her husband Joe, was all for it.

But, Lisa knew that she couldn't do all of the extra work by herself; she'd be exhausted all the time. So, she asked Joe to help with meals and the boys. He refused, saying that the house, the boys and yes, the job, too, were hers. No, he certainly wouldn't be doing anything extra at home.

Rather than be assertive with Joe and try to negotiate some kind of compromise, Lisa kept quiet. She knew better than to argue with him; Joe always won. He did it by silently, emotionally withdrawing from her. And, now that she had told him about the offer, she didn't dare refuse the job. She knew he was counting on the money, and he'd be furious if she turned the job down. She decided she would just have to work harder and longer to get it all done and keep him happy. And, that's what she did.

5. Pleasers are Over-Responsible.

If you're the Pleaser, you're "in" your partner's situation, busily handling whatever he needs to have done. In your busyness, you don't detach, stand aside and observe that your partner isn't "in" it, taking care of it himself, even though it's his problem/project. Why not? Your partner probably has the belief that he can do life the way he wants, regardless of its effect on himself, you or anyone else. Of course, he may not be aware of his inner belief; he's just bound to behave in the way he does.

His belief isn't a healthy one for him or you. But you, wanting the relationship so badly, can't allow yourself to let this reality into your awareness. No, instead you, the over-responsible person goes along behind your loved one, like a vacuum cleaner sucking up the emotional and financial junk that he has strewn about.

Here's an example. Your partner drives too fast and gets tickets often. He won't pay them, so you pay those you can. Before long, your partner must attend driving school, or do community service, or both.

You, the Pleaser, pick up the pieces of this continuing crisis. You call a traffic attorney to defend your partner. You pay his retainer fee. You show up in court when he won't. You put the driving school times and the community service schedule on his calendar. If you can't take him (his license has been suspended and so, he can't drive), you make the calls and arrange for his rides because he won't. After all, he believes he shouldn't have gotten the tickets in the first place. But, since he did, he falls back on a successful thought (belief) he has had during all of his past crises: "Someone else (you) will take care of it."

Here, the subject is your partner's irresponsible driving habits. But, we could be talking about any "content," such as, changing jobs frequently, not paying the bills, staying out until all hours of the night, drinking too much and not going to work, running up the credit cards, lying to you about how he's running his business, and on and on. The important thing is that no matter the content involved, the process remains the same.

215

You, the active, responsible one, feels responsible (yes, there's that word again) for taking care of your partner. You're so used to doing the "thinking through the problem, solving it, and then handling it," that you may not recognize the process you're in. That process: your loved one behaves irresponsibly and his lack creates trouble. You do what you have to do to make the situation right again, over and over. In this relationship, there is a silent, conscious or unconscious understanding between you that you will get it done.

6. Pleasers are Over-Understanding and Over-Accepting.

The Pleaser tries to understand thoroughly all sides of an issue or behavior. Because relationship is so important to him, he stays away from any kind of negative opinion. But, of course, while we should not judge others, we should not ignore the truth (real behavior) either.

The Pleaser refuses to see his partner as he is. Because the Pleaser refuses to evaluate his partner's behavior honestly, he cannot always see what kind of person his partner really is. So, it's easy for the Pleaser's partner to tell hard-luck stories and get by with it.

Let's look at Rachel again. Even though John's response to his own obligations was not something she should have accepted, she sympathized and rescued. Because she is completely understanding and <u>always</u> accepts his point of view, she reinforces John's bankrupt behavior.

By not setting any value on her time, her money, her help/service, or her love, by not questioning or challenging John, Rachel provides too much of a good thing. Her understanding, acceptance, sympathy, kindness and generosity start out as a positive gift to John and to the relationship, but, over time, they end up encouraging self-centered behavior. Neither Rachel nor John benefit in the long run, nor does the relationship.

None of us should support unhealthy behavior in others for any reason. When you, the Pleaser, do so, even unwittingly, you perpetuate the illusion that you and your partner actually have a relationship. Now, you see that when a partnership isn't mutual, it isn't a relationship. It's simply one person using another.

Rachel eventually realized this.

7. Pleasers are Naïve.

If you're a Pleaser you're probably pretty naïve. You trust people without any reservations. So, you always believe the best about them. That makes sense given your belief system and your need to be connected to others.

However, the naiveté is so strong in you that even when the person you love is mean, selfish, not responsible, cruel or absent, you cannot entertain, never mind accept, what his behavior means. Why is the truth so hard to believe?

Here's why. If you fully acknowledged his behavior, logic would demand that you talk with him about it. But, you know that if you assert yourself, you're risking conflict. The conflict may lead to emotional or physical separation. And unconsciously, you believe that you can't be separated from the one you love. At the thought of separation, you feel panic-stricken, and you believe that you can't go on without him. So, you solve this dilemma by letting go of your hurt or anger. Then, you do not have to confront him. For now, all is well.

Soon, though, the two of you start the same hurtful cycle all over again.

You see, it's understandable that you would insulate yourself from the truth that your partner has done something wrong or has harmed you. This lack of reality about the person you love is part of the Blind pane in your Johari Window.

How can you continue to see your partner as someone he isn't? Once you, the Pleaser, decide that you care for someone, you unconsciously assign good qualities to that person. This process is so common with Pleasing people that it has a name; it's called the "halo effect." That is, you assign

217

positives with little or no evidence that the good qualities you assume he has, are actually present. For example, you might conclude that because a person is attractive, he will also be friendly. Or, because a person is generous, you conclude he is also honest. Of course, these "assignments" may not be true.

Judy and Tom.

Tom, Judy's husband, complained about his job; she knew he wanted a change. He promised Judy, though, that he would talk with her before he made any move. Instead, he simply quit. And, he didn't have another job to go to.

Instead of seeking new work, he decided to go to graduate school, even though he had never liked college and had not been a good student. He told Judy that she'd have to go back to work fulltime. Judy, naïve and ever optimistic, assured him she would work while he did a graduate MBA program. Yes, she knew, way in the back of her mind, that he hadn't loved school his first time around, but she trusted that he would do graduate school differently. What was her thinking based on? Nothing but her wanting it to happen.

Taking a job meant that Judy wouldn't be able to stay at home with their three young girls, even though that had been their agreement before Tom quit his job. Her disappointment about this sacrifice was almost overwhelming. But, she wanted to give her husband this opportunity, and so she surrendered those precious moments with her children.

Two years later, Tom graduated from his MBA program. Of course, Judy expected that he would find a satisfying job, and then all would be well with their family. But, he didn't. He took quite a while getting a job. And then, he changed companies a couple of times in the next 18 months.

In spite of Tom's erratic behavior, Judy never complained about his lack of responsibility. She plugged along supporting all five of them, emotionally and financially.

Her friends all wondered how she did it; they wouldn't do it, they said. One day, Judy learned she wouldn't have to do it anymore, either. She came home from work to a note from Tom, and a house that had been stripped of possessions. He had left her for another woman he'd met in graduate school.

Lesson: If Judy hadn't been so naïve and trusting, she might have studied Tom more carefully. She might have questioned him about why he made the choices he did. What was he thinking, and what were the motives driving his behaviors? She might have asked herself if Tom acted gratefully or did he take her for granted. And so on. If she had known more about the meaning of certain behaviors, if she had been more watchful and thoughtful, she could have protected herself, and her girl's needs, much earlier. As it was, Tom cheated all of them.

8. Pleasers Don't Set Boundaries or Limits.

Each of us has an invisible cylinder of air around us. This is our personal space. We own it. We say who can or cannot come into it and when and how. People who aren't Pleasers not only understand this idea but they enjoy it and enforce it in varying degrees. People who are not Pleasers understand the concept of Separation. That is, each person does have private space that he has a right to manage.

The Pleasing person not only doesn't own this idea, but has probably never heard of it. And doesn't want to.

Further, if he did hear about it, he would reject it, symbolically and practically. That's because the idea of a personal space that's not open at all times in all ways to all requests from the one he loves goes directly against the Pleaser's core beliefs. His idea of connecting is to always be touching symbolically, intellectually, emotionally, and physically whenever possible. The Pleaser's idea of connection is to meld together so that you can't discern where one person starts and the other ends. Does the Pleaser know these things about himself? Not usually.

Sophie and Al

Sophie and Al married when they were both 44. It was a third marriage for each of them. Sophie's two previous husbands had been alcoholic, she, their classic enabler.

219

Al had two daughters, Alaina, a sophomore at the state college two hours away, and Hannah, a sophomore at the nearby high school. Sophie had two younger boys, Greg, 11, and Clay, six.

This particular Saturday, Al, Sophie, Greg and Clay drove south to Alaina's campus to watch the football game. The night before, on Friday evening, Sophie told Al that she wanted to drive down, eat dinner and drive back with all of them. But, she didn't want to go to the game.

The weatherman had forecasted rain for Saturday afternoon; she didn't want to sit in it for three plus hours. She thought she would spend her time shopping at the mall.

On Friday Sophie said that if it were not okay with Al for her to shop if it rained, she'd rather not go. She encouraged him and the kids to go on; she just didn't want to be wet and miserable all day. Al said "Okay" to the shopping.

Saturday morning it seemed that everything between Sophie and Al went okay. They got on the road. But, as they were driving Saturday afternoon, it began to drizzle. By the time they were halfway there, the rain was coming down steadily.

Sophie reminded Al that she was going to the mall while they were at the game. Right then, he started in on her. "What's the matter with you that you can't stand a little rain? You're so fragile (dripping sarcasm) that water is going to hurt you? You're a God-damned baby, isn't she?" turning to her boys in the backseat. "There's something wrong with you if you'd desert your husband and children for the God-damned mall. What kind of a wife and mother are you? We know, don't we boys, she's a rotten one."

The language and tone worsened with every passing mile. By the time they got to the game, she'd cried, off and on, for two hours.

Of course, he didn't drop her at the mall. He drove straight to the stadium. He ordered the boys to get out; he got out and the three of them began walking to the stadium gates. She called to him to leave the keys; he just laughed. She sat in the car through the entire game, immobilized, uncertain what to do.

Why hasn't Sophie set some limits? Well, actually, she has tried. How does he respond to her attempts? He ignores them, or laughs at them. Or he talks her out of them, or sometimes he puts on the "I feel sorry for myself because you're treating me so bad" act.

Does he take these boundaries seriously? No, because she never follows through on them. Why? When she's emotionally or physically separated from him, she feels lonely; she misses him. She's so dependent on the connection with him that the thought of being without him, alone, produces too much anxiety in her. So, she lets him back into her space: she starts talking to him again, sleeps with him, has sex with him, and once more, he becomes the center of her life.

Ellen and Dan.

Ellen and Dan went out for the evening with two other couples. On the way home Dan accused her of flirting with Joe, one of the other men. Ellen said she had no idea what he was talking about; he knew she never flirted. But Dan kept talking about it, insisting that she had embarrassed him with her teasing. They were almost home when, in the middle of a sentence, he backhanded her in the face. Shocked and hurt, she yelped and started to cry. That made him even madder and he started shouting at her to shut up. The second he pulled into the driveway, she opened the door and was out of the car and into the house like lightening. She ran up the stairs, into their bedroom and locked the door behind her.

A few minutes later, Dan went up to the bedroom expecting to get into bed; he was tired. But, he found the door locked. When he shouted at her to let him in, Ellen said she would, but only after she knew he had calmed down. After some more shouting about how unfair she was to deprive him of his bed, he left the door and she could hear his footsteps going down the stairs.

221

About a half-hour later, after she had gotten ready for bed, she opened the door quietly and went downstairs. She thought she'd find him watching television in the living room. Not there. Maybe he was in the kitchen having something to eat. Not there. As she came out of the kitchen into the hallway, she heard the bathroom door creak. She opened her mouth to tell him that she was sorry he felt upset, but she knew she hadn't caused it.

Ellen never got the words out. He slammed her up against the wall, knocking the breath out of her. She struggled to get up but he pushed down on her shoulders; she couldn't move. She tried to roll away from him at the same time she started screaming. And screaming and screaming.

Ellen's 11-year-old son, Donny, came running. He'd been asleep upstairs but now his mother's yelling awakened him. She was screaming: Call 911, call 911!! Scared to get in the middle of the two adults, he did what she said.

The police came, arrested Dan, took him to jail and put him in the holding cell. If Ellen would agree to testify against him, they would charge him with assault and battery within the next 24 hours. If not, they'd have to release him, if he could make bail.

Ellen didn't sleep well; she kept struggling with what to do. Her mind jumped back and forth: Dan was her husband; how could she have put him in jail? Well, husband or no, he had scared her and now she couldn't trust him. Wait a minute, didn't she owe him another chance; maybe there was something she could do to make this right. Yes, she had some responsibility here; if she didn't, why did she feel so guilty? And, she felt selfish, too, him in jail and her comfortable at home. Okay, okay, she'd make it right. She'd talk to him in the morning.

Ellen bailed Dan out the next morning on Sunday. The following Saturday night, six days later, when they went out with friends for the evening, they danced the same routine (process) all over again. Nothing had changed.

9. **Pleasers Avoid Confrontation.**

1. Sally hates the fact that her husband, Tony, has no friends and no desire to make them. This means that if they have any social contact at all, the planning and the contacts are up to her. Sally hates the fact that Tony has no goals of any kind, even work ones. She has to tell him how to do his life. This means that she has almost total responsibility for their family. But, will she confront him about any of it? No, because when she has in the past, he yells at her and even threatens. She's afraid of that Tony.

2. Occasionally, both Ralph and Peggy speak sharply to their three kids. When one does it, the other one doesn't like it. Peggy confronts Ralph about it but he won't confront her. Why? She's a quicker thinker than he is and more verbal. She's always ready with a defense. He's decided it's hopeless to confront her. No matter what he says, she always wins. She never hears him. He's afraid to speak up.

10. **Pleasers "Forget" Offenses.**

Watch the following line of thinking. If you, the Pleaser, quickly forget the injustice done to you, and rapidly let go of the feeling of hurt it caused, you don't have to confront him. If you don't confront your partner, you won't have conflict. If you don't have conflict, the relationship is not threatened. If your relationship isn't threatened, you don't have to fear that you'll be separated from the person you love. If you're not separated, you won't die from anxiety. Your anxiety can fall; you're safe in the relationship. Do you see why you "forget?"

Once again, you, the Pleaser, are driven to preserve your connection with that other significant person, no matter the quality. If this is you, stop the care-taking and start "doing" you. Think about it. If your life is consumed with solving other's problems, when do you do you? "Oh, I don't even think about that," you say. "That's the point," I say.

Recover your life and be grateful. You can.

✿ ✿ ✿

This is a fairly good list of Pleasing defenses but by no means is it comprehensive. There are many other common, but subtle, behaviors that are used to maintain your love connection. Look for them.

ॐॐॐ

All Defenses.

Once you get the idea of why defenses are used, you'll notice how frequent they are, even in daily living and in common conversation, never mind in a heated personal exchange. If you're at all interested in people-behavior, the study of defenses will fascinate you, and at the same time, boggle your mind.

ॐ   ॐ   ॐ

Big Ideas From Chapter Ten.

1. *The Pleaser's Beliefs.*

   A. *I need someone to love and/or I need someone to love me.*
   B. *I can trust people.*
   C. *I must feel sorry for others.*
   D. *I can't disappoint others, especially those I love.*
   E. *I am responsible for those I love.*
   F. *Whatever others need, I should supply.*
   G. *I must avoid rejection at all costs.*
   H. *I shouldn't ask for anything for myself.*
   I. *I come last; my needs are unimportant, certainly not as important as others, especially those I love.*

2. *The Pleaser's Defenses.*

   A. *Pleasers Accept Other's Excuses.*
   B. *Pleasers Over-Explain.*
   C. *Pleasers Lie For Their Partners.*
   D. *Pleasers Placate and Appease Their Partners.*
   E. *Pleasers are Over-Responsible.*

F. *Pleasers Over-Understand and Over-Accept.*
G. *Pleasers are Naïve.*
H. *Pleasers Don't Set Limits.*
I. *Pleasers Avoid Confrontation.*
J. *Pleasers Forget Offenses.*

Balance Your Pleasing Beliefs;
Give Up The Defenses.

225

*Can you let go and let life fall
as it must, naturally?*

ર   ર   ર

Chapter Eleven

Curing Defenses

*O*kay, what does it take for you to give up your defenses? First, decide that you want to let them go. Does this statement seem unnecessary? It isn't. Defenses are strong; they have a life of their own. To rid yourself of them, you must make a strong commitment to drop them. Further, you must want to be defense-free for your own emotional health, not just for your relationship.

Think about this carefully. Defenses have no value; they're destructive. They defeat you and any growth you want because they keep you closed. You originally grew your defenses to protect your beliefs, as a coat of armor might. But now, along with any threats to you, they also keep out any good that might come in.

To have good emotional health, give up anything that protects you from real life. You can't deal with reality if you don't know what it is. And, you can't know reality if you deliberately keep it out. When you don't cope with adult requirements in an open, positive way, you make your own reality. To whatever degree yours differs from the real world, you're on dangerous ground.

Further, to have an intimate relationship, you must give up anything that separates you from your partner. Since defenses are the most separating habit you own, it's important to let them go. Making this decision means you are free to use wonderful PROACTIVE, forward movement. Thankfully, it replaces old defenses, which are backward REACTIVE movements. Obviously, using open behavior, while initially more scary and difficult, is the only way to spend your life. Take the chance. Living without defenses will eventually bring you peace and happiness.

This decision to give up defenses is not an easy one. As you grasp what will happen if you drop your defenses, you might get scared. Here's what I mean.

When you give up your unhealthy beliefs and your defenses, your feelings are literally unprotected. Where the defenses were once, there is now an open space. This yawning hole is scary; it makes you feel completely vulnerable. And, on top of that, you feel as though your emotions are too large for you to handle. You imagine that your scaredness will take over. Panic may evolve to anxiety before you stabilize. You might want to back away from your decision because you are frightened; it feels so awful.

Pause here. Before you let that fear overtake you, realize that you can develop positive stuff to replace your old defenses. That empty space can be filled with self-awareness, new, healthy beliefs and life skills. All this because you've learned to:

1. examine your internal self,
2. pin down your feelings, beliefs, motives, conscious thoughts,
3. recognize when you feel defensive,
4. develop the discipline to wait,
5. talk with your partner respectfully.

But, right now, as you think about giving up your defenses, try to manage your fear.

☙☙☙☙

Taking Charge of You.

So, you've made your commitment to eliminate your defenses. Now, the question is: how?

228

You must observe your internal self. You're probably pretty aware of your outward behavior, but pinning down precisely where your defensiveness comes from, takes acquainting yourself with your feelings and thoughts. Focus inside on your feelings as they rise. (Remember, you can't progress without this inner awareness.) Yes, they come up when you FEEL threatened. You may not have actually been threatened. But, you feel that way.

You sense danger. Your guard comes up and you're ready to REACT. You may do this without even understanding what your partner is really saying. That's because by now, you're operating only on feeling.

Okay, you're aware: the defensive feeling has risen; it's in your throat. This is the decisive moment. You can act out your negative feelings as you've always done. Or, you can remind yourself that you've vowed to practice the following techniques every time you feel those awful feelings rise.

The Defense Cure:

1. Sit tight, don't talk, be quiet.

DO NOT REACT.

The next time you're feeling defensive, tune in to your internal atmosphere and notice the amount of anxiety you feel. It will be amazingly high.

Then:

2. Breathe deeply.

Deep breathing is great at a pressure time like this. Here's how.

Focus on your breath. Close your mouth. Inhale through your nose at a normal rate to a silent count of four. Hold the breath for eight seconds. Then, exhale very slowly through your mouth for eight seconds. Picture the numbers inside your forehead as you say them. Repeat this process as many times as you need to feel in control of you.

Emotionally, this kind of breathing calms you. Physically, this deep, concentrated breathing will literally change your body's heart rate (which increases when your defensive feelings rise), from super-fast to something more manageable. And, it will lower your blood pressure.

The reason deep breathing works is because it generates much more oxygen than we usually take in. The heart doesn't have to work as hard as it does when it must compensate for shallow breaths.

As a change, when you get really good at this kind of breathing, you may want to use a word or phrase that feels soothing to you, instead of counting. Saying your favorite prayer, or a line of poetry works here. Simply repeat it in rhythm with your breathing.

Then:

3. Focus on your thinking.

Notice the thoughts going through your mind at the same time you're feeling defensive. They're probably something like: a. He's attacking me, b. I must defend myself, c. I must take control, d. I must fight or he'll win, e. If I keep talking, he'll give in. And, so on. These thoughts are old childhood beliefs that you probably weren't aware were influencing you. But, they are. These irrational thoughts come into your mind, and they direct defensive talk or controlling behavior when you perceive that you're too emotionally, intellectually or physically vulnerable, that you're being attacked or being criticized.

So, you see, if you're going to communicate rationally and calmly, instead of just REacting, you must take charge of yourself. You can only do that by becoming more aware internally. Then, you must commit to yourself that you will develop inner discipline. Healthy behavior will gradually follow.

4. Next, try to assess neutrally (NOT DEFENSIVELY) the comments that are coming in from your partner.

Ask a question or reflect back to your partner what you think you heard to make sure you understand what your partner is MEANING. Resolve to do this WITHOUT DEFENSIVENESS. Gradually, this process will calm you.

5. Finally, when you think you can, WITHOUT DEFENSIVENESS, continue the conversation.

Seek to stay emotionally connected to your partner by understanding the meaning of what he is saying. Try again, CALMLY, to say your own feelings and thoughts. Practice this whole process over and over until it becomes automatic.

かくかか

Yes, this is the process you want to build. Some of these steps, like the breathing and counting, can be practiced easily when there's no threat. Try it while you're driving, while you're in the shower, or at your desk for a 5-minute break. Remember, the deep breathing is good for your body anytime, because it's calming. Further, if you practice this technique when you don't need it, it will rise automatically to help you when you do need it. Practice all of these steps, and then practice some more. You'll enjoy success if you do.

かくかか

Two Incidents.

Next are a couple of examples in which the partner of a defensive person stayed open and practiced the above process. These may encourage you to be patient with yourself and your partner as the two of you transition into new behaviors.

In the first case, Jim uses an active defense. In the next situation, Andrew uses a passive defense. Both Mary and Kathy were caught by surprise when their partners behaved in unexpected ways. That's part of why a defense is so effective so often for the owner; it surprises others. But eventually, if you get to know defenses well, you won't be startled by defensive behavior. It really is predictable.

Mary and Tim.

In this situation, the defense is aggressiveness. Remember in Chapter Seven, we discussed some of the verbal

231

games that are used for control. We said then that these communications could be classified as defenses because of the motives behind them.

Mary had finished getting ready to go out with her husband, Tim, and three other couples to a wine-tasting party. She'd chosen her outfit carefully: a long-sleeved, teal-blue dinner suit with a cream-colored silk blouse and a rose chiffon scarf. She wore a large six-carat diamond solitaire ring on her left hand, a smaller ruby ring on her right, a diamond watch and an elegant diamond necklace around her neck. She decided to go without a bracelet; it seemed like too much. All in all, Mary liked her look. She'd known for many years how much her appearance mattered to her husband, Tim, especially when they were out with other people. Because she wanted to please him, she was always extra careful about her appearance.

As she was picking up her purse and gloves to go downstairs to the car, Tim asked, "Well, where's that bracelet I bought you last week? You should be wearing it."

"I just thought it was too much with the rest of my jewelry. It will overwhelm my dress. And besides, too many pieces at one time make me feel gaudy."

"That's crazy! What kind of woman leaves a new expensive diamond bracelet like yours at home? Go put it on."

Mary, who had been walking across the room, now turned around, faced Tim, and spoke calmly, "Are you insisting that I wear the new bracelet tonight, even though I'll be self-conscious about it, and I really don't want to?"

"Damned right I am. Show the thing off!" Tim replied.

Mary hesitated; she studied Tim. "Okay, if it means that much to you, I'll wear it tonight." Mary's voice was not only calm but also understanding. (She had paused to calm herself and gather her thoughts). "But later, we'll talk about this conversation we've just had. I don't like the way you spoke to me. And, I don't like it that my feelings don't matter to you. I might even think that showing off the bracelet is more important to you than I am."

Tim, surprised, said, "What the hell does all that mean?" Mary's response was, "I'll go into it more later.   We really don't have time now."

In this dialogue, Mary used the healthy responses she had developed. Silently, she refused to argue with him, as she had always done before. Instead, she focused on her internal atmosphere, and practiced the steps she had learned to help her use self-control. Then, she shifted the focus of her comments to the process happening between them (that is, how he was talking to her).   Instead of just reacting and escalating the situation as she had so many times in the past, she tried to understand him. She also gave him more information about why she didn't want to wear the bracelet.   She decided to be assertive in the moment but not reactive.

In the past Mary had either argued or given in and tried to pacify him. Then, she would grumble and feel resentful about it. Giving in had always allowed her to avoid confrontation. But, over the years, she understood that her behavior had encouraged, not just Tim, but all those she loved to take advantage of her. They didn't respect her wants or needs. Because of that, she had a storehouse of resentment against them.   She was tired of the whole process.   She wanted something better now.   By dong it differently this time, she embarked on a new journey, one of being more true to herself, more honest. She preserved the evening, but promised herself and Tim, that later she'd talk about his controlling behavior.

Time out: let us step out of the content for a moment here   and   talk   about   process.   Both   staying   silent (submissiveness) and arguing (aggressiveness) are REactions that Mary had used with Tim in the past. Neither one worked. Both when Mary stayed silent, and when she argued, Tim reacted to her reactions. From that point on, their defenses fought with each other. When defenses fight with each other, nothing is resolved. True, the players stay safe behind their defenses, but there is no real communication happening, either. And most importantly, the relationship suffers.

233

0_____5_____10
Submissive   Assertive   Aggressive

Defensive   The Only Healthy Choice   Defensive
Combines
Openness, Directness, Honesty

Later, Mary got the talk she wanted. She said clearly that she wouldn't be bullied as he had routinely done for years. Now, she expected Tim to start handling himself better instead of dumping on her with controlling language. She expected him to talk to her decently. Were Mary's expectations reasonable? Yes, not only reasonable, but necessary for a healthy relationship.

Of course, Mary didn't get a shift in behavior from Tim that night. But, she <u>did</u> get his attention. Since that was more than she'd had in years, she considered it a good start. And gradually, over time, Tim calmed down, and learned to talk to her differently.

Her courage grew more every time she stood up for herself.

ॐॐॐ

Andrew and Kathy.

Andy and Kathy had planned a picnic with their three young girls one Sunday afternoon at a neighborhood park. As Andy put his fishing equipment in the trunk, Kathy said, "I didn't hear you mention that you wanted to fish, Andy. Is that what you're planning?"

He said, "Yeah, I thought today could be Becky's special "first fishing time" with me. Remember, I took Christy when she was six?" (Christy is their older daughter.)

"Yes, I remember, but when we talked about going to the park, you didn't say anything about wanting to take Becky fishing. If you were thinking of it for today, why didn't you mention it to me? Don't you think that Rachel, (their four-year-old), will be upset, seeing you go off with Becky? You know how she hates to be left out," Kathy said. John replied, "It didn't occur to me to bring it up. To tell you the truth, I didn't even think about Rachel. She might be upset, but you can distract her for me." "I don't want to distract her for you. I thought we were all going to spend our time together," Kathy said, "And, I've been looking forward to that." Andy didn't respond.

"Andy, do you realize this changes the whole afternoon's schedule? Brett and Molly are expecting us early this evening for dinner. The fishing takes more time; we'll probably be late." Then, Kathy said, "I wish you had mentioned it to me so we could have talked about it together." Andy didn't reply. And, he avoided looking at her.

"You didn't tell Becky you'd take her, did you?" Kathy asked. "Yeah, I mentioned it this morning," Andy replied.

Kathy drew a deep breath, "That <u>really</u> upsets me. You leave me completely out of the planning loop, but still you expect me to take on extra work. I resent all of it. It isn't considerate of our friends, either." Kathy exclaimed.

Andy's body froze, and he literally backed up, away from Kathy and the car. Kathy continued, "Andy, I really want you to put off the fishing. And from now on, please let me know ahead when you want to make plans that include me. At least then I'll feel like I have some say in it. And, when we plan the fishing for Becky, I can do something fun with Rachel, so that she won't feel left out." Andy nodded and mumbled, "Yeah," as he walked away.

In a hurry they finished putting the kids and the picnic things into the car. They went off to the park. Andy pulled into the parking area, and the girls tumbled out. He opened the trunk and unloaded things onto the ground. Kathy, the two older kids and the littlest one, Rachel, got busy carrying stuff to the picnic area.

A couple of minutes later, Kathy caught sight of Andy, with his fishing pole in one hand and Becky's hand in the other, heading down the park path to the pond. Obviously, he was taking Becky for her "first time fishing."

In confronting Andy a second time, Kathy used the same fairly healthy talk. Step I: To be sure she understood what was going on, she "checked out" her information. Step 2: Then she stated her feelings of disappointment and anger AGAIN about his going against the agreement they had made a second time at home. Step 3: She asked AGAIN for what she wanted: planning together and enough respect to follow through on agreements they made.

Let's look more closely at what happened. Andy had at least five unconscious beliefs that were operating in the original incident. First, I can do life the way I want. Second, I don't have to listen. Third, when others disagree with me, they're attacking me. Fourth, bad things will happen if I disagree with my partner. Fifth, I can handle situations by avoiding them.

The defenses Andy used to protect his beliefs were: (1) ignoring, and (2) silence. Let's look at the "ignoring" first. Andy heard Kathy's words, but since he didn't agree, he simply disregarded what she said. Because he's afraid to discuss issues, it makes sense to him that if he's going to do something and Kathy doesn't want him to, he should ignore her, rather than argue with her. It doesn't occur to him to give up what he wants or to negotiate. Remember, he has a belief that he can do what he wants (and besides, what could be wrong with wanting to take your daughter fishing?). You can see he's wholly focused on Content here, the fishing, not on the Process between him and Kathy. He's unaware that he treats her with disrespect when he (1) leaves her out of the planning, and then (2) uses her while he goes to do something he didn't allow her to plan for.

Another of Andy's beliefs is that when Kathy disagrees with him, she is attacking him. He reasons, again unconsciously, "I can ignore anyone who's attacking me. What I'm doing is not only okay, it's positive. After all, I'm doing something with my daughter." Again, he doesn't examine his Process (how the talk goes between him and Kathy). He focuses on the Content (the activity with Becky).

Next, Andy is thinking, "I don't want to change my plan with Becky, and yet, I can't argue with Kathy about it." Remember, Andy has a belief that bad things happen if he argues with his partner.   So, he reasons that silence (his defense) will work for him here.   But, by keeping silent, Andy doesn't allow Kathy to participate in decision-making.

It's clear by now, that Andy doesn't have any depth in his view of partnering.   He knows about <u>CONTENT</u>, (the everyday activities of life), but he seems truly unaware (no belief structure) about the partnering <u>PROCESS</u>.

He's a victim of his own "black and white" thinking.   He only sees that he (1) must go ahead and take Becky fishing (in which case, he gets his way), or (2) he does not take Becky fishing, and therefore, Kathy gets her way.   Unfortunately, he sees many situations in life from this "black and white," "win or lose" position.

By contrast, a healthy partnering process would include setting goals together, consistent "checking in" with each other about schedules, and discussing it all to reach a compromise position, it there isn't immediate agreement.   This partnering process is what Kathy is focused on.   She's correct.   In the picnic situation, she would have been glad to work Andy's fishing into their schedule, but not in the way Andy approached it.   Partners include each other in their process.   Instead, Andy excluded Kathy.

Healthy relationships are done through cooperation, not competition.   Healthy relationships include communication: sharing ideas, gathering information, if necessary, and then, cooperating to set goals and find solutions.   Healthy relationships include negotiating, decision-making and problem-solving together.

Andy's whole process is a "loner" one.   He decides what he wants and does it without consulting his partner.   Even though he is married, he operates as though he is single; he stays out of the communicating and negotiating parts of the relationship, while at the same time, can reassure himself that because he's married, he has a relationship.

By behaving the way he did, Andy prevented connected relationship from happening. In good partnering, Andy and Kathy would TOGETHER talk, plan, negotiate the day and then, TOGETHER experience the satisfaction and warm closeness that comes from both people talking to each other, being heard and working it out. Not having done that, he didn't get satisfaction or intimacy. But, he got his way.

And, what about Kathy? Every time Andy does this, she feels betrayed. Then quickly, anger rises because it happens often. Her negative feelings pile up and don't always go away. It's a high emotional price to pay.

Clearly, this marriage would be much better if Andy would give up his unhealthy beliefs and the defenses that protect them, so that he could have a smart, loving relationship.

ﮩﯿﮩﯿﮩﯿ

From Defensiveness to Self-Awareness to Self-Control to Self-Confidence.

The old saying that "practice makes perfect" has something to it. If you want to be defense-free, you must become aware of your inner process. How? Develop awareness by constantly, vigilantly watching your own behavior. To accomplish watching, be "present" to yourself moment to moment. To do so, notice your thoughts as they pass through your mind; name feelings as they come up inside you. Practice.

Once you are aware of your own behavior, your goal is to move from Reactive behavior to proactive, thoughtful action. As you practice, you will begin to choose moments where you sacrifice feeling comfortable now (just spitting out words is always easier than disciplining yourself to sort your feelings and thoughts), for feeling satisfaction later (gradually taking control of your mouth and actions). Little by little, you're choosing responsible behavior.

As you forego short-term reactions, gradually, you build discipline and self-control. So, continually look past the "now" moment to the future. Self-control results from persistently training yourself.

On first tries, you may frustrate yourself. But have the courage to keep trying. Don't despair when you don't see immediate change.   Respect the strength of your original personality beliefs and their defenses. Remember, they are powerful; it is difficult work and demands consistent practice. You will prevail only if you persist.   Thoughtfully choosing to act toward a particular end takes more time. But, every time you do so, you are developing self-control. You are leaving behind your defensiveness.

New healthy habits develop as practice continues disciplining yourself. Self-confidence emerges as you increase your self-control.   As your self-confidence grows, you trust yourself more and more to behave proactively in a positive way. You're developing a new healthy process.

Over time, you realize that you have acquired a deep core of inner strength. Congratulations. You deserve it; you've worked for it. Enjoy it.

ॐॐॐ

The Smart, Healing Process.

I promise you this. Do the "Defense-Cure," and good things will develop for you.   If you diligently, everyday, EVERYDAY, practice the remedies we've discussed: discovering your beliefs, dropping your defenses, communicating well, and so on, these new processes will be automatic when you need them.

Expect that these new movements won't feel natural to you when you first begin to use them. You'll feel uncomfortable, and it will take some time to be at ease with them. Don't be discouraged if you aren't immediately successful. Keep trying. They become natural as you practice.   Your payoff?   You experience a great feeling of sureness; YOU'RE FINALLY IN CONTROL OF YOU.   Further, you bring healthy, smart stuff to your relationship.   When your partner does the same, that intimate relationship you've been working for is yours.

The Defense Cure:

1. DECIDE to be defense-free!

      Remember that your defenses have a life of their own. They are very old and very sturdy and will not want to give up their power easily. Be determined.

2. PRACTICE slowing down your responses.

      Feelings and words come up and out of your mouth before you know it and before they should. Breathe ...... and think your way to calmness.

3. WAIT.

      You don't have to speak now. There will always be time for you to say what you need to say. Practice patience. WAIT.

4. FOCUS on your feelings. Become aware.

      They are your feelings; they reside in you. You own them. You are responsible for knowing them well enough to identify them. You are responsible for speaking them in a respectful and non-threatening way. They are YOUR feelings. Don't blame others for them. Your partner has his own set of feelings. He's probably struggling with his, just as you are with yours.

5. FOCUS on your thoughts. Become aware.

      Listen to your thoughts in these crunch moments. They are a sample of your childhood beliefs. These are YOUR thoughts. You are responsible for knowing them. You are responsible for sorting the positive ones from the destructive ones. You are responsible for speaking the good ones in a respectful, non-threatening way. You are responsible for filtering out hurtful, threatening, dark thoughts. AWARENESS here is critical.

6. LISTEN to what your partner is saying, without defensiveness.

You have chosen him to be the most significant person in your life. Honor him by suspending your own internal busyness. Quiet your inner self: LISTEN.

7. SHARE your feelings and thoughts, when you know them, calmly and openly, without defensiveness.

Remember, you have chosen this person to be your life partner. You are responsible for telling him who you are in an assertive but calm way. Develop patience. Develop trust in yourself and in your partner. Then, your intimacy will deepen.

8. ENJOY the results of your inner work.

Celebrate the good that comes from your Relationship work. You've earned it!

ॐॐॐ

At Last: Peaceful Living.

This is the essence of self-esteem: (1) knowing yourself well (your feelings, your beliefs, your motives, your defenses, your styles), (2) using healthy behavior and skills to meet the ceaseless demands of the real world without defensiveness, (3) firmly expressing yourself in respectful positive ways, (4) Then reaping the reward: solid calmness and internal peace. And, even though it's difficult at the start, it's worth the work. It will benefit you through the rest of your life. I urge you to try it.

ॐ   ॐ   ॐ

Big Ideas From Chapter Eleven.

Cure Defensiveness:

1. *Do not react.*
2. *Breathe deeply.*
3. *Focus on thinking.*
4. *Listen to your partner.*
5. *Continue conversation calmly.*

Two Cases:

> *Mary and Tim*
> *Andrew and Kathy*

Go from Defensiveness to Self-Confidence by increasing your Awareness and Self-Control.

Practice The Defense Cure:

1. *Decide to give up your defenses.*
2. *Practice slowing down.*
3. *Wait to speak.*
4. *Focus on feelings.*
5. *Focus on thoughts.*
6. *Listen to your partner.*
7. *Share what you know about yourself without being defensive.*
8. *Enjoy the results.*

Give Up All Defenses;
You'll Be Glad You Did.

Chapter Twelve

Relationship

Connecting Is The Prize;
Let's Put It All Together.

*O*kay. You've embraced many new ideas. Let's very briefly condense them.

Personality Types.

Your Inner Work. The four personality types operate differently. Familiarize yourself with the profile of each style. Strive to understand each of them and how they affect your life, either because you or others you love own them.

Develop your strength to deal strongly and competently with yourself and what life hands you. Choose not to complain about who you are not and how awful life has treated you. If you feel weak, it's only because you have some unhealthy, nonproductive beliefs. You can change those. Call up your courage and your energy to do it. If you feel incompetent, it's only because you lack some life skills. You can get those now; they're yours for the effort.

If you own negative beliefs, drop them. Begin immediately to build new healthy ones. Make this important commitment to yourself. Why? Negative thoughts dampen your spirits and generate pain. Don't allow that. Instead, grow new, productive beliefs. Then, experience calm and happiness.

Relationship. Now because you know the personality types, you understand how you and your partner are different. If you view this as a problem, please don't. Instead, see yourselves as complementing each other. This is one of the positive, though probably unconscious, reasons why you chose each other. If you accept this view, you get a whole new appreciation for your partner.

Balance. Remember, emotional health is balanced behavior. Strive for it. When you aim for individual healthy wholeness, you create two separate, strong people ready to share life with each other. It is much different than the dependency you might be experiencing now. It feels clean; it feels wonderful. So, make healthy shared intimacy your goal.

᠀᠊᠀᠊᠀

Communication.

Practice level, respectful talk. Show love by understanding, reflecting, checking out, and so on. Eliminate vertical talk: judgments, hidden agendas, sarcasm, etc. A relationship can't flourish or even hold its own with that kind of talk in the air.

Talk deep talk. To build a closer relationship, practice talking with your partner at deeper and more exposed levels. Reveal your feelings in your talk and ask him to do the same. If you do this process, your disclosing should go well and being together should feel better for both of you.

᠀᠊᠀᠊᠀

Respect.

You view and accept your partner as a person of worth without criticizing, judging or depreciating him. Respect includes an acceptance of your partner's faults and deficiencies, as well as his positives. Because you respect him, you feel a deep interest and concern for his growth. You show it. You realize respecting, accepting and loving a person does not mean agreeing with or condoning all of his behaviors. He gives you the same gift.

Respect is many things. It is an __attitude__ you have toward yourself and others. It's a __feeling__ you get from and give to others. It's __action__ that shows care about your own and the other person's feelings and thoughts and situation. Because it is all of these, there's no substitute for this gift of Respect to each other.

Defenses.

The Glass Wall. Now you know how defenses separate you from others in your life. But, especially with your partner, defenses prevent closeness. They keep you emotionally apart from the one you love. They keep you lonely, solitary. Use the Defense Cure to cleanse yourself of useless defenses. Then, be grateful they are gone.

৵৵৵৵

Conclusion.

Good relationship begins when two people who like and value each other come together. If love and commitment are to deepen, each partner must be as unselfishly interested and invested in the other as he is in himself. Each person must have the goal to develop positives that will enrich not only his own life, but also the life of the other. When healthy beliefs, attitudes and behaviors are present, each person values and respects himself and gives value and respect to the other. In this atmosphere, each is emotionally, intellectually and physically safe. Each contributes. Each knows that he is wanted. Each can give and receive knowing that there is equality and balance between them. This describes healthy, emotionally safe relationship.

Separately, Relationship, which is the character of the connection created by two people, has a life of its own apart from the two people experiencing it. These two people must each be as invested in the growth and in the endurance of the Relationship as each one is invested in his or her own desires and goals. The life of the bond, the Relationship, which they nurture between them, depends on their mutual investment.

So, if you want your Relationship to flourish, honor it in these ways:

1. Develop the beliefs, feel the attitude and show the behaviors of Respect.

2. Vow to eliminate any competition between you and your partner. Loving Relationship prospers with cooperation, negotiation and conciliation.

3. Learn and use level, respectful communication. Eliminate the vertical, controlling kind.

4. Understand your partner's styles as complementing your own. As you come together to make a whole, you get what you originally partnered for: a truly intimate togetherness called Relationship.

Do these attitudes and processes guarantee a life free from difficulty? No, life will always present its problems. But the processes do guarantee two people ready and able to successfully partner through difficulty and come out on the other side of it, whole, strong and committed to each other.

〜〜〜

My Best Regards and Good Wishes to you as you journey your own special path to health and thus, freedom and peace.

〜〜〜

Write me; I'd love to hear where you are in your journey. More information about many of the concepts in the book is coming. Thanks for your interest.

Appendix A

Values

≈ Referred to in
Chapter 5 ≈

As Tom put on his coat to go to work that morning, Paula said: "You know, last night's conversation hasn't ended, at least not for me. We need to talk." "You can talk all you want, but I'm not going to look at other jobs; I like the one I've got." "Tom, we need more income; your job doesn't bring in enough." "It would be plenty if you didn't spend every dime you get your hands on for clothes and house junk." "You mean, it would be enough if you didn't insist on both kids going to private schools and taking lessons in everything they can think of." Tom said, "I want the kids to have those opportunities. I guess you don't feel the same way." "No, I don't. I believe in the public school system. I came up that way and I've been successful." Tom cut in, "I see we don't value the same things." Paula said, "Maybe we don't."

In his last remark, Tom put his finger on the cause of the argument between them: each valued different things. So, you might ask, exactly what are values?

Simply, a value is defined by what you'll spend your personal resources on: your time, your money and/or your energy. Your values show in your behavior and in what you own.

Maybe you already know what you want to own; what you like to do and how you want to behave.

If you don't know, though, the list of possible values below will help you recognize what you are already acting out. Choose those qualities, actions and things that define you.

If you need other ways to clarify your values, you can ask yourself how you feel about everyday decisions you must make. Your values will show up in your answers.

1. Is career advancement important to me? Will I spend my time, energy and money on it?
2. Do I want to own a home?
3. If so, how do I want to furnish my home, simply or extravagantly?
4. Do I want order and organization in my home or doesn't clutter bother me?
5. Do I want to have children?
6. Do I believe in raising children strictly or leniently?
7. Do I like an active social life with friends or do I like my free time with only family? Or, do I like to be alone?
8. What activities do I spend my free time on when I'm alone?
9. Do I know what will make me happy?

Money (income, possessions)
Competition
Status (social position)
Success (outward)
Image
Saving money
Sports (any kind, watch or play)
Dancing
Board Games
Music (listen or play)
Travel
Entertainment (of all kinds)
Theatre
Education (personal growth, career, interests)
Reading

Intimacy with others
Respecting others
Taking care of others less fortunate
Relationships
Children
Family (original, extended)
Friends
Fidelity
Solitude
Safety
Honesty
Fairness
Kindness
Generosity
Conformity
Independence

Appendix A - Values

Privacy	Freedom
Animals	Peace (in family,
Commitment (to people,	in world)
to action)	Courage
Environment (protecting it)	Responsibility
Humor	Hard work
Trust	Self-growth

Have you ever found yourself in a value conflict, having to choose from two things that are both important to you? For example, you might value both career and time with your children. You'll become very aware of how much each means to you if you must allocate how many hours or days to spend on each.

Here are some fairly common personal conflicts. Where do you go on vacation: to Colorado for skiing or to New York for the theatre. How do you keep your pet comfortable while you're gone? Several of your values might be in conflict here. They are money: what will give the most value (paying a neighbor, paying a kid to dog-sit, paying a kennel) versus your pet's comfort: (what will he like the most), and your peace-of-mind. Which is most important to me: my value on physical fitness to stay healthy or graduate courses that will help me advance in my job?

You can see, just from these few examples, that situations arise often where you must choose one of your values over another. Knowing yourself makes these choices less confusing and makes you a better partner.

෩෩෩

Appendix B

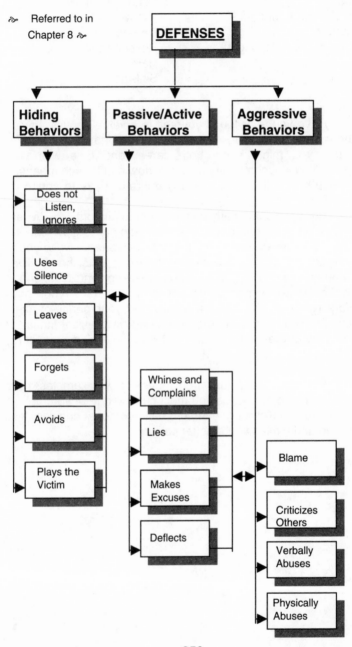

Appendix C

Index of Book Characters

Chapter Two

Joan
Erika
Shannon
Ed and Nancy

Chapter Three

Claudia
Toni and Lisa
Emma
Tom and Lydia
Al and Joy
Bill
Kathy and John
Jennifer and David
Jeffrey and Jan
Alex
Lisa and Norma

Chapter Four

Stephanie and Jim
Todd, Sara, Adrienne and Betty
Michael and Beth
Eric, Jan and Joel

Chapter Five

Michelle and Bob
Claudia and Ron
Clark and Sophie
George and Julie
Rudy and Hannah
John and Anne
Sam and Amy

Chapter Eight

Chris and Jeanne
Brad and Paige
Mary Ann and Blake
John and Lisa
Emily and Jim
Tony and Hope
Mac and Joanne
Diane and Joe
Ken and Faith
Vicky and Patrick
Todd and Rebecca
Linda and Mark
Mary and Phil
Kevin and Kelsey
Joe and Ellen
Greg and Anne
Susan and Mick
Tom and Beth
Marilyn and Bryan

Chapter Ten

Rachel and John
Lisa and Joe
Judy and Tom
Sophie and Al
Ellen and Dan
Sally and Tony
Ralph and Peggy

Chapter Eleven

Tim and Mary
Andrew and Kathy

Glossary

A

Acceptance. An open attitude and behavior. Giving unconditional respect and empathy.

Active listening. The ability to listen to another person with complete attention to what he says and, more importantly, means. Empathic listening in which the listener echoes, restates, and clarifies.

Adlerian Therapist. A person who uses individual Psychology as the foundation for treating emotional illnesses.

Adlerian Therapy. A psychotherapy which seeks to influence an individual's lifestyle.

Aggression. Pushing toward one's goals without respect for others or the situation, and despite opposition.

Anxiety. The response to unreal or imagined dangers. An emotional state of fear and apprehension. The anxiety interferes with direct and effective solutions to real problems.

Appease. To calm or pacify, to reassure, especially by granting demands.

Argue. Resist what is being said. To debate, to engage in a dispute. To bicker, fight, quarrel.

Assumption. To decide what is true without proof. Supposition.

Attitude. The state of mind and/or feelings about something or someone—can be positive or negative.

Avoid. To dodge, evade, elude, to stay clear of, to shun.

B

Balance. To stabilize, neutralize. To make equal or level or steady or even.

Behavior. Everything we do that can be directly observed. Any act, movement, or response of a person.

Belief system. A collection of internal statements, ideas, about oneself, others and life.

Belonging. The person's yearning for acceptance by the members of his group: family, school, job, etc. To belong is to find a place in his current group.

Birth Order. In a family, birth order refers to being an only child, a 1st, 2nd, 3rd, 4th and so on, child.

Blame. To hold someone or something at fault. To censure, charge, condemn, criticize, denounce.

C

Comfort. Anything that feels good. Rest, quiet, relaxation, gratification, luxury, warmth, plenty, creature comforts, satisfaction of bodily wants, coziness, pleasure, happiness, contentment, restfulness, exhilaration, excitement. Out-of-balance need for comfort can produce addiction.

Communication. The receiving and/or sending of information. The conscious and unconscious movements one uses to make communication with others easier. Includes facial expressions and body language.

Complain. To express feelings of dissatisfaction. To bellyache, gripe, grouse, whine.

Compromise. Good faith bargaining, granting concessions, give and take, finding a middle course, finding a middle ground, negotiating.

Confrontation. When it's done well, it acknowledges a stressful situation directly and attempts to find a neutral solution to the problem. Meeting face-to-face, encountering to accomplish fairness. When it's done poorly, it consists of opposing, disputing, arguing, fighting.

Consciousness. Attention to ongoing inner and external perceptions, thoughts, and feelings. Alertness, cognizance, mindfulness, awareness, knowledge.

Control. To hold in check. To constrain, master, command, manage, instruct, supervise, govern. Can control self, situations, others or any combination of these.

Core Beliefs. The most primary and important beliefs a person owns.

Criticize. Judging adversely, censuring.

D

Defenses. Individual reactions designed to alleviate anxiety and maintain a person's feelings of worth and correctness rather than cope directly with reality, the stress situation. Unconscious method used by the psyche to solve problems and to protect the core self against unpleasant situations or impulses. Defense mechanisms will lessen or avoid stress by denying, falsifying, or distorting reality. The person's method of reducing anxiety by unconsciously distorting reality. Defenses deceive their owners to keep them comfortable.

Deflect. To turn aside; in relationships it is used to change the subject, used as a defense.

Denial. Allows a person to protect the self from reality by refusing to let the happenings of reality into his conscious awareness. Refusal to acknowledge a painful or threatening reality. Denial is acted out with a specific defense.

Depression. Low feelings, such as despair, despondency, sorrow, unhappiness, gloom, dejection, melancholy, misery, mortification, worry, discouragement, dispiritedness, hopelessness, distress, desperation, desolation, dreariness, heaviness of spirit, dullness, downheartedness, woefulness, disconsolateness, melancholia, darkness, disheartenment, dumps, doldrums. Many negative feelings, that overwhelm their owner.

Disposition. Temperament. A person's characteristic way of thinking, behaving and reacting.

E

Early Memories. One-of-a-kind memories about specific incidents, usually before seven or eight years old.

Embarrassment. To feel self-conscious or ill-at-ease, to feel disconcerted, confused, mortified. The feeling that the Control Type tries to avoid.

Emotion. Complex state of feeling involving conscious experience, internal and overt responses. Has power to motivate the person to action. Feeling or affect that involves a mixture of physiological arousal (rapid heart beat, for example), conscious experience (thinking about being in love with someone, for example), and overt behavior (smile or grimace, for example).

Empathy. The ability to understand and feel what another feels, to put oneself in someone else's shoes.

Encourage. Genuine support (words or actions) that lifts our mood. To inspire with courage and/or hope. Promotes progress.

Excuses. Various explanations for not being responsible. A defense used by all four personality types.

F

Family Atmosphere. The mood in the home. For example, the mood might be suppressive or materialistic or over-protective, argumentative, calm, positive, and so on.

Feedback. Telling the sender of a message just given what the receiver's understanding of it is.

Feeling. State of a part of the body. Sensitiveness, perceptiveness, consciousness, responsiveness, awareness.

255

Synonyms are: taste, emotion, passion, tenderness, sentiment, affection, judgment, sympathy, empathy, imagination, intuition, keenness, sharpness, spirit.

Feeling talk. Speaking about feelings to another. A must-have to achieve intimacy.

Friendship. A form of close relationship that involves (1) enjoyment (we like to spend time with our friends), (2) acceptance (we take our friends as they are without trying to change them), (3) trust (we assume that our friends will act in our best interest), (4) respect (we think our friends make good judgments), (5) mutual assistance (we help and support our friends and they us), (6) openness (we share experiences and deeply personal matters with a friend), (7) understanding (we feel that a friend knows us well and understands what we like), and (8) spontaneity (we feel free to be ourselves around a friend).

Forget. To not remember, to not attempt to, to neglect. All four personalities use this defense.

G

Genuineness. Open sincerity, real, authentic talk and behavior. Not hypocritical or misleading.

Gossip. Talk about others in a personal or sensational way. One who gossips is someone who habitually spreads sensational or intimate facts.

Greeting. Initial words to another person upon meeting.

H

Head Talk. Opinions, concepts, thoughts, ideas, views, impressions, conjectures, assumptions. Excludes feelings.

Hidden Agenda. A hidden purpose behind a message or action that is only known to the sender.

Humiliation. To injure the pride or dignity of another person.

I

"I" sentences. The sender's feelings or thoughts put into statements that begin with "I". This language increases self-awareness and self-responsibility.

Identity. A person's understanding of the various aspects of himself. This understanding answers the question "Who am I?" One's sense of self. The result of a person's blended integration of his view of himself, his self-concept, his social role, his intellectual qualities, his values.

Ignores. To pay no attention to; to disregard. To pretend not to hear or see a message. A passive defense.

Insight. The ability to perceive the true or hidden nature of things, a perceptive observation. A sudden and often novel realization; the opposite of unawareness.

Interrupt. To speak when another person is speaking.

Intimacy. The result of one's ability to develop close, loving relationships. Experiencing intense intellectual, affectionate, sexual, emotional, and/or spiritual relationships with others. In Erikson's theory, the ability to form close, loving relationships, which is the primary developmental task of early adulthood. The quality of genuine closeness and trust achieved in communication with another person.

J

Judge. To hold a negative evaluation. Can also be an assumption, a supposition.

L

Leaves. A person "leaves" another person or the situation physically, socially, intellectually, emotionally, or any combination of these.

Lies. An untrue statement made deliberately; a falsehood. A fib, an untruth.

Lifestyle. The pattern of beliefs, motives, cognitive styles, values and coping techniques (defenses) that promote the behavior of a given individual and give it consistency. The way of life that reflects a person's choices and values.

Listening. To hear. The process of interpreting and understanding the significance of what someone says.

Listen Actively. With body, face and words, the listener shows interest and involvement. Listener reflects his understanding of speaker's feelings, beliefs and intentions. Feels and shows empathy.

Long term. A long number of years, as opposed to a short time period. Example: A 10-year bank loan, as contrasted with a 12-month bank loan.

Love. A strong, intense, passionate affection for another person. The feeling of attraction that may arise from sexual desire. To enjoy another.

M

Meaninglessness. The feeling that the Superiority Type person tries to avoid. To feel as though there is no purpose for living.

Misbelief. An unhealthy idea that isn't productive for its owner.

Mixed Message. When a person sends two or more different, usually contradictory messages about the same subject. Speaking conflicting messages simultaneously, e.g., one message verbally and another nonverbally at the same time or in close proximity.

Motivation. The internal reason(s) we behave as we do. A term used for the "why" of behavior; that is, why we behave the way we do, or why we do the things we do.

Motive. Cause, reason, purpose, behind behavior. A goal lies behind all behavior. Answers the question, "Why?"

N

Naïve. Unaware. Not worldly or sophisticated. Simple, ingenuous.

Nurture. Giving emotional care and support to another. To help grow or develop, sometimes through training or education.

O

Open. Not covered or concealed. Accessible, available, vulnerable. Exposed, uncovered, unprotected.

Over-Accepting. An exaggerated form of openness.

Over-Explain. To clarify and give the reason for an action in an exaggerated way.

Over-Responsible. Too dependable with duties or obligations. Sense of ownership to "get it done" is exaggerated.

Over-Understanding. Too much compassion and tolerance exhibited in an exaggerated, even naïve way.

P

Partner. A person who joins with another in a shared activity.

Passive Defenses. Behavior that stands still or moves away from relationship with another. Behavior that protects unhealthy beliefs.

Personality. Enduring, distinctive thoughts (beliefs), emotions, and behaviors that make each individual unique and that persists over time and across situations. An individual's distinctive and consistent patterns of thinking, feeling, and acting.

Personality Formation. Happens within first four to five years of life. It is the development of the self, which forms from a combination of heredity and environment.

Personality Type. A group of unconscious and conscious beliefs that direct an individual behavior into specific patterns. These individual collections of patterns are called personality types. Those identified in this book are: Comfort, Pleasing, Control, Superiority.

Physical Abuse. To physically harm or injure another.

Placate. To soothe the temper, to yield, to appease, to soften.

Pleasing. To give pleasure to. To gratify, satisfy, make up to, to be agreeable, delightful, pleasant.

Pleasing Defenses. Listed individually with explanations in Chapter 10.

Present. Fully concentrating, focusing, connecting.

Pressure. An urgent requirement. A distressing or oppressive burden. The feeling that the Comfort Type tries to avoid.

Process. How something gets done. The various steps that occur between initiating action and reaching a goal.

R

React. Thoughtless behavior, which is automatic.

Rejection. The feeling that the Pleasing Type tries to avoid.

Relationship. Connection, association, tie, affinity, link, kinship, bond.

Reporting Talk. To deliver information. To describe, narrate, provide details of, give an account of, inform, advise, communicate, summarize, make known, give the facts.

Resistance. Tendency to resist uncovering of repressed material in therapy; also tendency to maintain maladaptive behavior or symptoms and resist treatment. The therapy term for the client's unconscious defense strategies that prevent him from recognizing reality.

Respect. To honor, esteem, prize, cherish.

Romantic love. The type of love that has strong components of sexuality and infatuation; it often predominates in the early part of a love relationship. Love at first sight, based on the ideas that there is only one true love and that love is the most important criterion for marriage.

◆ Glossary ◆

S

Sarcasm. To ridicule, sneer, mock, show contempt.

Security. The feeling of being safe against loss of status, of friends, loved ones, income, or other needs.

Self. The central core in the personality around which experience and actions are organized. The core belief system.

Self-acceptance. Satisfaction with one's attributes and qualities while remaining aware of one's limitations; does not negate striving toward self-improvement and personal growth.

Self-actualization. The process of developing one's cognitive, intellectual, emotional, social and physical potential. The process of becoming all that one is capable of becoming, of developing a unique self, motivated by a need for continual growth, not merely survival.

Self-Awareness. To have conscious knowledge of what we are thinking, feeling, doing. Also to reflect upon, review and reevaluate aspects of our own experience.

Self-concept/self-image. The individual's sense of his or her own identity, worth, capabilities, and limitations. Self-concept refers to an individual's overall perceptions of their abilities, behavior, and personality. The person's perception of "who he or she is." All our thoughts and feelings about ourselves which answer the question, "Who am I?"

Self-Discipline. The person directs himself in goals, procedures and conduct within clearly defined and appropriate boundaries.

Self-esteem. Feeling of personal worth. Respect for and acceptance of oneself as a whole individual. One's feelings of high or low self-worth.

Self-talk (self-statements). The soundless, mental speech that is used when one thinks about something, plans or solves problems, and that is often very helpful in cognitive restructuring.

Short-Term. Something that occurs over a shorter time rather than a longer time, such as a week instead of a month.

Significant Other. Referring to any person who is very important to the individual, typically beginning with the individual's parents.

Silence. Absence of sound. Explained here as a defense. Person uses silence to indicate lack of involvement.

Social Interest. An attitude of "at-homeness," "belongingness," with mankind. Adlerian Psychology uses this term synonymously with altruism.

Stress. The response of individuals to the circumstances and events, called stressors, that threaten them and tax their coping abilities. Physical, mental, or emotional strain or tension, the cause of which may be psychological or physical. The whole process by which we perceive and respond to certain events, called stressors, that we appraise as threatening or challenging us.

Superiority. Higher, better, preferred, above, finer, of higher rank, a cut above, more exalted, excellent, supremacy, preponderance, advantage, perfection.

T

Temper Tantrum. Consists of inappropriate words and/or actions that aim to control another person or situation.

The Johari Window. Concept of a person. Consists of four areas: Open, Private, Blind, Unknown. Describes levels of self-disclosure. Describes self-awareness.

U

Unconscious. Lacking awareness. According to contemporary research psychologists, information of which we are unaware.

V

Values. Attitudes and judgment about what is important, desirable, and right to the individual.

Verbal Abuse. To verbally harm or injure another person.

Vertical Talk. Describes two kinds of talk: (1) Up-down – when a person speaks to another from a superior or controlling top position to a person in an "inferior" place, (2) Down/up – when one person speaks to another from a self-pitying, "less than" position to a person that he sees as more powerful.

Victim. One harmed or killed by the act of another by a circumstance or condition set up by another.

W

Whine. To protest or complain in a childish, irritating way.

Index

L

M

N

O

P

Order Form

Fax Orders: (636) 256-7954. Send this form.
Credit Cards accepted.
E-Mail Orders: smartrelations@att.net
Postal Orders: Evelany Publishing, PO Box 485
Ballwin, MO 63022. USA.

Quantity	Book	Price	Total

Name: _____

Address: _____

City: _____

State: _____ Zip Code: _____

Telephone: _____

E-mail Address: _____

Shipping:

US: $4.00 for the first book and $2.00 for each
additional product.

International: $9.00 for first book, $5.00 for each
additional product.

Payment: ( ) Check   ( ) Visa
( ) MasterCard

Card Number: _____

Expiration Date: _____

Signature: _____

270

◆ <u>Notes</u> ◆

• <u>Notes</u> •

◆ <u>Notes</u> ◆